THE LAST FRONTIER

Volume 42, Sage Library of Social Research

SAGE LIBRARY OF SOCIAL RESEARCH

The Last Frontier

The Social Meaning of Growing Old

ANDREA FONTANA

Preface by FRED DAVIS

Volume 42
SAGE LIBRARY OF
SOCIAL RESEARCH

SAGE PUBLICATIONS   Beverly Hills   London

For information address:

SAGE PUBLICATIONS, INC.
275 South Beverly Drive
Beverly Hills, California 90212

SAGE PUBLICATIONS LTD
St George's House / 44 Hatton Garden
London EC1N 8ER

Printed in the United States of America

Library of Congress Cataloging in Publication Data

Fontana, Andrea.
   The last frontier.

   (Sage library of social research ; v. 42)
   Includes bibliographical references and index.
   1. Aged. I. Title.
HQ1061.F59   301.43'5   77-23186
ISBN 0-8039-0832-6
ISBN 0-8039-0833-4 pbk.

FIRST PRINTING

CONTENTS

*To Tina for her steadfast support
in helping me understand*

PREFACE

That there are powerful, unchallenged, massively constraining and often inconsistent notions abroad in the land about what it means to grow old, what the old are like, and what happens to them is a recognition which has only recently surfaced from its prior state of pristine cultural embeddedness. At long last it has, thanks to studies such as *The Last Frontier,* moved into that at once eerie yet strangely illuminating crepuscular realm where what *was* no longer seems quite so, where new threads and connections suddenly reveal themselves among once apparently disparate objects, and where—most frightening and fascinating of all—the very act of perception itself is called into question. Can it indeed be that what was so surely out there and "known" about the elderly, that what you, I, and all other sensible folk took as given, just, right, and proper was mostly, as with so much else in social life, in the eye of the beholder? And, because our power to behold the thing is so inseparably joined to the thing itself, can it further be that were we to behold the aged differently, they, and later we, could be made different? But is the new beholding of those who one day we are to become, a mere act of will, a "saying it is so makes it so"? And, if not, what in their or the world's being would cause us to summon the act of will which once manifest, could alter the conditions and prospects of their own and our being?

It is to this elusive, enigmatic, intricately dialectic interplay of perception and conception, being and becoming, existing and beholding that fashions the lives of the elderly in our society that *The Last Frontier* so nicely addresses itself. It does so at a number of different levels and from different vantage points. First, by constantly juxtaposing one or another sociological theory of aging and leisure to the views and feelings of old people themselves, we come to see how the former are too frequently but overly elaborate extrapolations of questionable folk stances and nostrums concerning the elderly. Thus the familiar folk conviction that the old want to be by themselves and do not wish to be burdens on others finds its apotheosis in the late fifties and sixties in what came to be known as structural-functional disengagement theory, a "best of all possible worlds" formulation, which held that not only was this functional (read "good") for society, but it was what the old genuinely wanted for themselves as well. Without altogether discounting this reassuring form of moral absolution dressed up as scientific theory, Fontana shows how its applicability is limited, and then only in some special restricted sense to but a few of the many elderly informants he interviewed and observed, i.e., to the group he designates as "the relaxers," those capable of "disengaging" from the cares of their prior working lives for pleasures and diversions too long deferred or unexplored. Similarly, the familiar nostrum widely trumpeted by folk philosopher and huckster alike, that "you're only as old as you feel" and that "to stay young you've got to keep busy," finds more than its echo (a chorus of praise would be apt) in the activity theory of aging so widely accepted in the late nineteen-forties and -fifties. Here, too, Fontana finds that whereas this applies in part (again with certain ironic qualifications not foreseen by the theory's originators) to his "do-gooders" and "joiners," it barely comes to grips with the great diversity of life styles and outlooks he found among the elderly he studied.

Indeed, one of the distinct virtues of the approach taken by Fontana in this book is that without superimposing received sociological theory or concocting new conceptions a priori, it allows the old to speak for and be themselves. This serves the dual purpose of not only testing, clarifying, and adjudicating the dominant sociological theorems extant in the field, but of showing how, despite living lives animated in many instances by other than conventional values and meanings, the old are given, at the level of ideology and verbal opinion, to repeating much of the popular *and* sociological wisdom propagated about themselves. And it is this dynamic contradiction of an as yet relatively undefined altered life experience with the overly defined conventional representations of it that will in time generate new cultural meanings of aging in our society and new sociological perspectives on the aged. Because his ethnography is sensitive to the openness of the issue, to its never quite resolved and ever emergent character, Fontana's effort must be placed in the forefront of this quest for new vocabularies and outlooks which can better serve the aged and us in whose midst they live.

And, it is not merely of academic interest that Fontana and other open-minded social researchers like him succeed in the quest. For not too far off, with the "coming of (retirement) age" of the post-World War II baby boom—at roughly the year 2010, assuming our crudely chronological conception of retirement remains as unrealistic as it is today—with the decline in the birth rate to less than population replacement levels, with increasing automation, scarcer natural resources, more varied forms of leisure, and more diverse familial arrangements through the phases of the life cycle (e.g., later marriage, more divorce, more group living, and communal child rearing)—with all these changes, and yet others that defy anticipation, the existential meanings of age and aging are likely to be stretched and strained to where current definitions may seem as quaint and anachronous as that of the Chinese patriarch or the Puritan elder. Without the lively insights and open-ended methodology of works like *The Last Frontier*, which refreshingly render problematic much that society takes for granted, we are destined to remain ill-prepared for the onrush of this new old age.

Fred Davis

ACKNOWLEDGEMENT

This book has been so intertwined with my life in the past four years that it is difficult to remember the many people who reached out and helped me. However, I wish to thank everyone who stepped in and out of my life during these years for they helped me construct my manuscript, in one way or another. I especially wish to thank all of the old people who so patiently let me peer inside their lives. I am also indebted to Margaret Mead, whose reference to old people as "immigrants in time" inspired the metaphor of my title.

Those close to me deserve a special mention. Bennett Berger and Joseph Gusfield provided invaluable intellectual guidance and practical counsel. Jack Douglas molded my approach to the study of human beings. Murray Davis sharpened my wits to the nuances of everyday life. John Johnson anchored my dreams in obdurate reality. Lynne McEuen lent her expertise on the subject matter. Susan Sterner and Coleen Carpenter valiantly typed my work. Dennis Noesen patiently waded through early drafts. Lars Jensen insightfully edited the manuscript. Tom Sosnowski, Robert Kaplan, David Rumelhart, Patti Adler, Fred Preston, and Ron Smith lent their help. And above all my wife, Tina, without whose precious help and support this would not have been possible.

To all I say thank you.

Chapter 1

INTRODUCTION

This is a study of old people and their daily lives. Old people live by grasping on to what they have learned, on to what they believe, on to what they would like to believe.[1] It is the intent of this work to examine some of these beliefs by seeing how a particular segment of the American people, the elders, flesh their daily life with meaning.

Social scientists and society at large worry about the elders as poor, but they should look at the elders as elders, for they too shall be old one day. Poorness tints the elderly in the grayish color of age and grime, of deprivation and hunger. But what of the gates of retirement from a work-dominated life from which all shall pass? The fear of those gates looms large but unspoken for many people. When one thinks of growing old, one fears that past those gates all that will be left will be but to gaze at wastelands of emptiness, to lead a life devoid of meaning, assailed by the ageless fear of waiting, of waiting for nothing, of waiting for death, of waiting for waiting itself.

The thought of thoughtless days is not unusual as man has been troubled by the quest for the purpose of being over the centuries. This quest has taken different directions and different emphases at different times. In recent days it has ranged from the deeply religious searching of one's Christianity in Kierkegaard[2] to the defiant stance of man in front of the unknown in Nietzsche.[3] One may find the deep-seated fear of meaninglessness at the end of life, as exemplified by Tolstoi's character Ivan Ilych:

> Maybe I did not live as I ought to have done, it suddenly occurred
> to him. 'But how could that be, when I did everything properly'?[4]

Or one may struggle through existential pangs early in life as in the case of Jean Paul Sartre.[5] Do the essential features of man's being determine his actions as Heidegger affirms,[6] or do man's actions in the world determine the basis of his being?[7]

Sociologists have taken less ethereal approaches than philosophers in looking at individuals in this world. They have focused on the social features with which human beings paint the existential wasteland of human existence in softer and more pleasing colors.

Various sociological theories have explored the extent to which man imbeds the meaning of his life in the various structures of society,[8] and while they by no means agree on the nature of this structuring, there exists a general consensus that man crowds his life with preestablished normative meanings which allow him to proceed relatively undisturbed through his existence.

Bennett Berger[9] suggests that in order to see how steeped in social norms people are, one may wish to examine those periods of individuals' lives in which they apparently are free of normative constraints. Berger suggests that a study of leisure activities could reveal whether indeed leisure is free time that allows people to pursue their true interests, or whether the ways in which they employ their resources in leisure activities reflect a deeply ingrained socialization that direct behavior toward expected and socially proper conduct in which individuals feel they "ought to engage," thus making leisure the most constrained time rather than the freest time of life.

Following Berger's suggestion this author considers leisure and leisure time as excellent areas in which to study how people fill the time they call their own. However, while most people's leisure time is strictly budgeted,[10] there is a group in American society which is free from social controls and practical constraints such as the bondages of work,[11] raising a family, paving the way for future generations, etc. This group is the elderly.[12] Thus in studying how old people find meaning in their lives this study should be able to gain a better understanding of how people in general[13] make their lives meaningful when the rigid social structure which guides them through life is loosened. By so doing what should emerge is how much of a naked self is left when the clothing which gives it form is stripped away and just how much of that self is but the clothes.[14]

Theories on the aged are not very successful in aiding research on the meaning of old age for a variety of reasons. First, theories on growing old tend to be presented by scholars subscribing to different paradigms[15] and are formulated as diametrically opposed to each other, thus adding to the disorientation of the field since various sets of data seem to support and contradict each theory. Some theorists have observed that in the later years of life the ties that hold people to society become looser.[16] Others have stated that old age lacks a clearly defined role, leaving the elders with no clear prescriptions and proscriptions with which to face the rest of their lives.[17] These studies present different speculations as to the effects of the loss of stringent social norms upon the elders, ranging from that of carefree elders[18] to that of anomic figures.[19]

Second, the theories on the aged either present a large body of ethnographic data and invoke heuristic value for their studies[20] or present theoretical speculations unsupported by any data.[21] The studies which incorporate both theory and data fall prey to another mistake. They confuse the topic of inquiry of their study with the resources needed to conduct it.[22]

By this it is meant that in studying growing old, theorists tend to assume, at least implicitly, that they "know" what constitutes successful aging since they provide a series of values and measurements as indicators of this. Thus, what began as the unknown topic, growing old, has become the resource by which to conduct the study itself.

Third, both theorists of leisure and students of aging tend to make the same assumption: Leisure is activities. This assumption forecloses other possible ways to seek leisure[2 3] and creates a strong bias in favor of active old age in many studies. Finally, by assuming an unproblematic notion of leisure, studies on the aged eliminate an extremely important variable in determining the meaning of old age for the elderly themselves.

This statement of the problems in the current studies of the aged has brought to the surface some of the tasks of this study. Rather than choosing any theory a priori, all of the major theories on aging will be used for their value in explaining the meaning of growing old. Also, this work will attempt to minimize the confusion between topic and resources in the study of the aged and leisure by letting the meaning of growing old emerge through the daily practices of the elderly. Theoretical notions about the aged will be derived from the data themselves thus "grounding"[2 4] the theory.

I quickly discovered empirically the importance of small daily routines in determining the meaning of life for social members. In one of my first excursions into the field, while sitting out of the cold, windy rain in a musty recreation hall, I asked a grubby, amorphous, gray man how he spent his leisure time now that he was retired. Grandiose theoretical thoughts shattered in a slow-motion explosion as I witnessed the drama of a man whose meaning in life was to eat at least once a day and to sleep in bus depots while avoiding policemen's harassment. He was not in the recreation hall to dance or sing, but to sneak out a cup of coffee when nobody was looking.

The intention of this work is not to become enveloped in the straitjacket of criticism or to become so abrasive and pungent that it is but the tragic foretelling of a modern Cassandra, pointing to mistakes and stifling constructive efforts.[25] Rather, this work wishes to understand old people. It begins by briefly outlining the differences between physiological aging and the social determinants of growing old. Chapter 3 examines the various ways in which leisure can be viewed. This is no empty exercise in theoretical expertise but a necessary stepping stone to see the portraits of old people which follow. If the meaning of growing old through leisure pursuits is what this study seeks to elucidate, then an understanding of leisure is necessary before proceeding to the unknown frontier: old age.

Chapters 4, 5, and 6 rely on ethnographic data gathered through in-depth interviews and participant observation to examine the elders.[26] Research in these chapters spans a period of three years in different settings. Chapter 4 studies middle- and upper-class elders in and around a senior-citizen center. Chapter 5 explores lower-class elders in a metropolitan setting. Chapter 6 presents data obtained in a convalescent center to show the effects of institutionalization on growing old.

I chose not to limit my inquiries to a single setting although this is the approach usually taken by the few brave who decide to research old people through participant observation. These researchers usually choose a small community which provides a well-bounded setting for their study.[27] In this setting the people are usually nice, middle-class old ladies,[28] who are polite to the researcher and who can discuss their life-situation in a coherent fashion. But something is amiss this way. People also grow old in less gracious surroundings. There is nothing like talking to an old down and out "wino," while whiffs of acid breath, Ripple vintage 1974, overpower the researcher and fend off the ghost of old age for the subject. There is nothing like attempting to support the weary limbs of an old woman, while she shakes uncontrollably, a helpless victim of Parkinson's disease.

The concluding chapter draws together various theoretical implications from the data. Hopefully, it will be shown that the theories on the aged are not "rival" theories, but that they explain different facets of growing old, thus really belonging

together as subparts of a general theory on growing old. Studying retired individuals will also provide information about the
meaning of life through leisure pursuits, thus reversing the normal trend of life-meaning through work.[29] Finally, what old
age means to different groups of elders will be discussed: to
elders that see themselves as free from social bonds and seek
free expressions of their selves, to elders that fear the freedom
from social bonds and create new ties to regulate their lives,[30]
and to elders that do neither but just sit, waiting for the end to
a life by now void of meaning.

NOTES

1. For a classical statement on the discrepancies between means and ideal values,
see Robert K. Merton, "Social Structure and Anomie," in *American Sociological
Review* 3 (1938): 672-682. For a more direct statement on discrepancy between the
situation of the elders and the conditions of society see Irving Rosow, "Old Age:
Moral Dilemma of an Affluent Society," in *The Gerontologist* 2 (1962): 182-191.

2. William Barrett, *Irrational Man.* Garden City, N.Y.: Anchor, 1962.

3. F. Nietzsche, *Il Meglio di F. Nietzsche.* Milano: Longanesi, 1956.

4. Leo Tolstoy, *The Death of Ivan Ilych and Other Stories.* New York: Signet
Classics, 1960: 148.

5. Andrea Fontana and Richard VandeWater, "The Existential Thought of Jean
Paul Sartre and Maurice Merleau-Ponty," in *Existential Sociology,* Jack D. Douglas
and John Johnson, eds. New York: Cambridge University Press, 1977.

6. Laszlo Versenyi, *Heidegger, Being, and Truth.* New Haven, Conn.: Yale University Press, 1965.

7. Jack D. Douglas and John Johnson, op. cit.

8. They range from the rigidly structured functional theories to the drama-
turgical approach of Goffman. For example:

> The waiter in the café plays with his condition in order to *realize* it. This
> obligation is not different from that which is imposed on all tradesmen. . . .
> There are indeed many precautions to imprison a man in what he is, as if we
> lived in a perpetual fear that he might escape from it, that he might break
> away and suddenly elude his condition.

Jean Paul Sartre, quoted in Erving Goffman, *The Presentation of Self in Everyday
Life.* Garden City, N.Y.: Anchor, 1959: 76.

9. Bennett Berger, "The Sociology of Leisure," in *Work and Leisure,* Erwin
Smigel, ed. New Haven, Conn.: College and University Press, 1963.

10. See Chapter 3.

11. Throughout this volume, work will be used to signify the activity in which
one engages to support oneself and for which one receives remunerations. See
Sebastian de Grazia, *Of Time, Work, and Leisure.* Garden City, N.Y.: Anchor, 1962.

12. Throughout this work elderly, elders, seniors, old people, oldsters, etc. will be used to identify a particular segment of American society. Others refer to them only as "old" people, see Arlie Russell Hochschild, *The Unexpected Community.* Englewood Cliffs, N.J.: Prentice-Hall, 1973. Hochschild claims that to use anything else than "old" softens the term. But, after all, as Shakespeare's Juliet so aptly told Romeo: "What's in a name? that which we call a rose, by any other name would smell as sweet. . . ." Thus, if members of society prefer to use a variety of names rather than the dreaded "old," so shall we in this work.

13. The popular claim that "old people are different" since they are preoccupied with death is largely a myth. This author found in his research that old people are more aware of "dying," seen as the practical concerns over one's demise such as will, cemetery plot, life insurance, powers of attorney, etc., but that only a few of them are more aware of "death" than other age groups; death meaning the existential realization of one's impending doom.

14. See Erving Goffman, op. cit., for a notion of self as a prop; also see Georg Simmel, *The Conflict in Modern Culture and Other Essays.* New York: Teachers College Press, 1968, for a discussion of the conflict of life versus forms.

15. Thomas S. Kuhn, *The Structure of the Scientific Revolutions.* Chicago: University Press, Second Edition, 1970.

16. Elaine Cumming and W. E. Henry, *Growing Old: The Process of Disengagement.* New York: Basic Books, 1961; Elaine Cumming, "Further Thoughts on the Theory of Disengagement," *International Social Science Journal* 15 (1963): 377-393.

17. Irving Rosow, *Socialization to Old Age.* Berkeley: University of California Press, 1974.

18. Elaine Cumming and W. E. Henry, op. cit.

19. Irving Rosow, op. cit.

20. See, for example, the ethnography of Jerry Jacobs, *Older Persons and Retirement Communities.* Springfield, Ill.: Charles C Thomas, 1975.

21. See, for example, Elaine Cumming, "Further Thoughts on the Theory of Disengagement," op. cit., in which the author herself, after a brilliant theoretical excursus concludes by stating that: "I have taken what is for me the pleasanter alternative of thinking widely rather than rigorously."

22. The original formulation of topic and resources departs much more radically from sociological concerns than our interpretation of it. See Don Zimmerman and Melvin Pollner, "The Everyday World as a Phenomenon," in *Understanding Everyday Life.* Jack D. Douglas, ed. Chicago: Aldine, 1970.

23. See Chapter 3 in this work.

24. Barney Glaser and Anselm Strauss, *The Discovery of Grounded Theory.* Chicago: Aldine, 1967. Also, for an excellent empirical study which lets definitions emerge through members' procedures, see David Sudnow, *Passing On: The Social Organization of Dying.* Englewood Cliffs, N.J.: Prentice-Hall, 1967.

25. For a recent criticism of "Cassandra-like" methodologies, see Lewis Coser, "Two Methods in Search of a Substance," American Sociological Association Presidential Address, 1975.

26. Names of research subjects and of locations in which research was conducted are fictitious.

27. See, for instance, Jerry Jacobs, *Fun City: An Ethnographic Study of a Retirement Community.* New York: Holt, Rinehart and Winston, 1974.

28. See, for instance, Arlie Russell Hochschild, op. cit.

29. For sociological theories dealing with internalized controls, see Weber's ascetic puritans in Max Weber, *The Protestant Ethic and the Spirit of Capitalism.* New York: Scribner's, 1930. Also, see the inner-directed man in David Riesman, *The Lonely Crowd.* New Haven, Conn.: Yale University Press, 1961.

30. A different notion of the everpresent social constraints is furnished by Sherri Cavan in her study of bar behavior in San Francisco, Sherri Cavan, *Liquor License.* Chicago: Aldine, 1966. Cavan looks at "time out" in bars during which an individual should be free from social obligations and restraints from the world outside of the bar. But it would seem that one is held accountable for one's behavior at any time, thus "time out" is not really time out at all.

On the same topic, Stanley Parker, in his book *The Future of Work and Leisure,* New York: Praeger, 1971, quotes from T. Yukawa on industrial recreation and makes the point that "time out" is really used by firms to assess the leadership qualities of the employees while they are "off guard."

Chapter 2

THE PROBLEMATIC NATURE

OF GROWING OLD

Well, I thought it would be dramatic if there was an old man around while they were packing the pictures. A poor old man, trying to get a job helping them. But they can't use him — he's in the way — not even as cannon fodder. They want strong young people in the world. And it turns out he's the man who painted the pictures many years ago. [1]

Is this what old age is all about? The arid feeling of a parched life nearing the end. Although the futility expressed by the Fitzgerald quote is not at first sight visible when we examine various sociological theories of growing old, it reflects a deep and generally felt concern in American society with the abhorrent fate of becoming old in a passive fashion. [2]

Old age exists, but just what this elusive notion comprises is not clear. Growing old cannot be easily defined or measured. This ambiguity may stem from either of two causes. The first cause, popular among most gerontologists, is that since gerontology is such a new discipline[3] we still lack the proper amount of data, both theoretical and empirical, to reach a satisfactory definition of the process of growing old.

While it is indeed true that gerontology is but a new-born baby among other disciplines, there is a second cause which

accounts for the ambiguity of providing definitions when dealing with growing old. The problem resides with the complexity
of the notion itself: Growing old is a problematic, complex
process, everchanging and continually being influenced by many
factors. Thus one may be condemned to rely upon a loose
definition rather than attempt to solidly nail down a stable
concept.[4]

It will be shown later in this work that various sociological
attempts to provide definitive statements about the process of
growing old have fallen short of the mark. And it must be so,
since the mark is an intangible and moving target.

Before coming to the problem of defining old age, we must
face and attempt to clarify the confusion present in the literature between the notions of aging and of growing old. While implicitly understood to be different, the two concepts are often
loosely interchanged, thus creating unnecessary confusion.

Aging is a life-long process, largely physiological, to which
we are all inexorably subjected. Some of us may attempt to
retard aging, forestall it, correct it, but it ruthlessly carries on.
Growing old is socially determined by the matrix of one's economic, industrial, and social complex, by one's own decisions;
it is the seeing oneself as "old," and being so labeled[5] by others
at some time of one's life.

Aging

When gerontologists proudly reveal that aging begins at birth,
they are, according to Irving Rosow,[6] presenting a socially
meaningless statement. Rosow states that to speak of aging
from birth ignores the difference between growth and decline
in life, and it also confuses physiological conditions with social
norms and expectations. Although Rosow is right, he over-
looks that indeed aging begins at birth, but that what usually
is referred to as aging is really intended to mean the process
of growing old. Unless this difference is clarified, to speak of
aging as a life-long process is meaningless when referring to the
later years of aging, since it collapses the differences between a

particular stage of our life: growing old, with the total span of our existence: the process of aging.

Aging is the process, largely physiological, whereby a body grows and then declines in a trajectory which figuratively resembles a bell-shaped curve. The declining part of the curve is characterized by losses in bodily functions[7] which cause a body to age.[8]

Few studies focus directly on aging itself when examining physiological processes. Thus, in dealing with aging one often must be content with the "by-products" of more generally oriented research.[9] A close examination of the aging process would be well beyond the scope and interest of this work, thus it will only provide a cursory look at aging.[10]

The physical changes faced in the descending years of the curve of life are many. An important one is the diminishing level of immunoglobin. This tends to lower the immunities to illness thus accounting for a lessened ability to withstand disease in the elders. Another important, often dramatic change concerns skin, which becomes rough and wrinkled. Dark spots of pigment can usually be observed. The skin loses hydration and thus its suppleness and flexibility.

Other changes occur as ocular functions decrease causing cataracts and glaucoma. Hearing losses are also common. In the later stages of the aging process, joints tend to stiffen, particularly hips and knees. Compressed spinal discs produce a bent posture. Hardening of blood vessels create circulatory problems in the brain, while the respiratory, digestive, and reproductive systems all tend to decline. The three major diseases of the later years of the aging cycle are heart ailments, arthritis, and arteriosclerosis. Intellectual changes are also noticeable. Aged individuals tend to become forgetful and make more errors of commission[11] than younger subjects.

All of the factors mentioned above and many others contribute to the reduced physiological functioning of human bodies[12] and can be seen as part of the aging process. But aging by itself does not account for growing old.

Growing Old

Being old is the last stage of our lives, but there are no clear markers to indicate the transition into old age. Then when do people see themselves as old?

Ernest Burgess points to the evidence[13] supporting chronological age as the social determinant of being old. He states that in European countries the most common age of compulsory retirement from the labor force is sixty-five. The choice of this particular age finds support in the statistical data of European countries of Western culture: Life expectancy at birth for males in thirteen European countries is sixty-five years.[14]

Burgess is well aware of the arbitrariness of choosing a particular age as the coming of old age and he is even more aware of the arbitrariness of selecting chronological age as the main social determinant of old age. To wit: "[Sixty-five is] the arbitrary age at which aging may be said to begin. . . . In the future we undoubtedly will have a better criterion than that of chronological age."[15]

Other sociologists have pointed to the problematic nature of age-grading. Havighurst, for instance, suggests an approach to the elders in terms of social competency and flexible adaptation to new roles.[16] Wayne Dennis[17] indirectly shows the absurdity of relying on chronological age by examining the productive years of scholars, scientists and artists. He finds that the productive output of scholars such as historians and philosophers continues in their seventh decade of life just as strongly as it did in their third decade. Scientists, on the other hand, show a marked decline in productivity in the later years, while artists begin their production earlier but decline much faster than the other groups.

Bennett Berger goes beyond the notion of productivity and suggests that different groups may be seen by others and see themselves in terms of the cultural generation or occupational group to which they belong.[18] Thus, being young or old has little to do with chronological age, and one could be an old Ph.D. candidate at thirty but a young professor a successful year later, as Berger suggests.[19]

Parsons and Platt in examining the socialization of students raise the question of retarding entrance of youth into the role of adults.[20] Any group will experience, according to Parsons and Platt, unrest when their socialization process is extended, giving rise, in this case, to a troubled period called "studentry." Changes in the social structure are thus seen as extremely important in determining the social behavior of a group of people.

Leo Simmons' study of seventy-one different preindustrial groups[21] clearly shows the functional place occupied by older individuals in the social structure of their societies. Irving Rosow employed the data of Simmons' study to compare the social structures of the preindustrial societies with that of modern-day industrial America.[22] He thus showed the different treatment of the elders by societies with different values and institutions.

Older people could maintain some social function in low-productivity economies, as some tasks for the elderly could always be found given the societal need for any help that could be obtained. The technological and industrial development of American society brought about serious consequences for the elderly.[23] It largely eliminated the opportunities of employment for the elders because the rapid technological change made their knowledge obsolete.[24]

At the same time our society shifted from one of mechanical solidarity to one of organic solidarity.[25] This change led individuals to become more independent and self-reliant while decreasing the amount of mutual dependence among societal members.

Industrialization also brought about a growing reliance by American society on meritocracy, coupled with the impersonal efficiency of bureaucratic systems.[26] Laws regulating compulsory exit from the labor force were instituted, and society provided benefits for individuals who retired.[27]

Social security was, however, only a supplement to the income of retired people. The individual was to enjoy the later years of his life by relying on the savings and pensions which he had carefully planned for and put aside. He was supposed to be the primary provider for the years of retirement.

A paradoxical situation began to arise. Older individuals in the United States found themselves caught between the American credo of self-reliance and individualism on the one side and the notion that they are entitled to a happy retirement regardless of their economic strength on the other. Thus financial means should be provided by governmental agencies, when needed. This, of course, leads to socialized care for the elderly which contradicts American values of individualism.

Growing old should be the last stance of individualism,[2][8] as the aged, modern-day Davy Crocketts, explore the last frontier: old age. But what if the means to go at it alone are not there? What if efforts to preserve individualism are thwarted by the lack of available jobs,[2][9] by empty bank accounts,[3][0] by the ostracism of the rest of the populace,[3][1] by the lack of social roles which will befit old people,[3][2] by governmental social policies of institutionalization for the elders?[3][3]

The choice is not simple, and many avenues are open to the aged. They may go at it alone regardless of handicaps and refuse "charity," living in the gray, damp, crumbling hotels downtown, sleeping late to avoid thinking about breakfast, making tomato soup with catsup and hot water under the disapproving eyes of cafeteria attendants[3][4] and pilfering small goods from department stores.[3][5]

But this choice may prove too demanding. People may give in to social pressures, in different ways. The crunching blow of failing health may irremediably curtail one's individualistic efforts by requiring hospitalization or extended care by others.[3][6] The invisible iron hand of depression may lead some people to forget their trouble by lifting a bottle and often lifting their freedom as well, as "concerned" people institutionalize them.[3][7]

The elderly may themselves come to believe that they are worthless, second-class, hopeless, destitute, and act as if they were. They may respond to stereotypes about the aged by complying with them thus becoming what a sociologist has referred to as "cultural dopes."[3][8] They may tip-toe unobtrusively in dark corners, sadly believing that their frail, hesitant figure should not disturb the bold path to glory of the young.[3][9]

Products of a consumer society, the elders come to believe that they are obsolete products and suffer the fate reserved to old cars and broken plastic toys: They are discarded.

Old people, at times, refuse to be thrown on the junk pile to wither away. That fate, they would agree,[40] is all right for other old people, but they do not see themselves as old. They close their eyes to the signs of aging on their faces, to the wrinkles, the gray hair, the drooping jaws, and other visible markers. If old age is a social label, many old people refuse to accept it. Significantly, both my own data and studies by others find a high incidence of elders who provide self-reports as young or middle-aged.[41] But if the "others" around them refuse to confirm their definition of themselves then the aged migrate to havens for the elderly, to Sun City, Golden Hills, Whispering Palms, to places where the denial of other groups is but a faraway whisper. There they have each other to reinforce their belief that they are still young.

Old people's life becomes a trip down the rabbit hole. They can believe in Humpty Dumpty, in talking rabbits, in the Queen of Hearts,[42] they can even believe that they are still young, as long as they all agree on it, as long as they have no blue-eyed, lean, tanned-bodied, freckle-faced youngster around to remind them that what they see in the mirror is a mask that society labels as old.[43]

NOTES

1. F. Scott Fitzgerald, "A Man in the Way," in *The Pat Hobby Stories.* New York: Scribners', 1970, p. 16.

2. See Chapter 3 in this work, especially the part on the work ethic.

3. Formal interest in the aged did not begin until the 1940s. The Committee on Social Adjustments in Old Age was established by Dr. E. Burgess in 1943, the Journal of Gerontology began publication in 1946, etc. See Clark Tibbitts, "Origin, Scope and Fields of Social Gerontology," *Handbook of Social Gerontology,* Chicago: University of Chicago Press, 1960.

4. See the Appendix, especially the discussion of G. H. Mead and M. Kuhn.

5. For a discussion of labeling theory see Howard Becker, *Outsiders.* New York: Free Press, 1963.

6. Irving Rosow, *Socialization to Old Age,* op. cit.

7. Arthur Schwartz, "A Transactional View of the Aging Process," in *Professional Obligations and Approaches to the Aged,* Arthur Schwartz and Ivan Mensh, eds. Springfield, Ill.: Charles C Thomas, 1974.

8. The aging of our body does not per se make us old, but rather the conception of ourselves that we derive from the aging signs.

9. Clark Tibbitts, op. cit. Even works like *Normal Aging II,* Erdman Palmore, ed., Durham, N.C.: Duke University Press, 1974, which provide a compendium of articles on aging, include many essays in which aging is not the focal concern.

10. In our discussion we rely on Erdman Palmore, op. cit.

11. D. Arenberg, "Changes in Memory with Age," *The Psychology of Adult Development and Aging,* C. Eisdorfer and M. P. Lawton, eds. Washington, D.C.: American Psychological Association, 1973.

12. Many losses attributed to the elderly, however, are myths, such as the loss of sexual interest and capacity. See, for example, Isadore Rubin, *Sexual Life After Sixty.* New York: Signet, 1967.

13. Ernest Burgess, "Aging in Western Culture," *Aging in Western Societies,* E. Burgess, ed. Chicago: University of Chicago Press, 1960.

14. Ibid., p. 5.

15. Ibid., pp. 5-6.

16. Robert J. Havighurst, "Flexibility and the Social Role of the Retired," *American Journal of Sociology* 59 (1953-1954): 309-311.

17. Wayne Dennis, "Creative Productivity Between the Ages of 20 and 80 Years," *Middle Age and Aging,* Bernice Neugarten, ed. Chicago: University of Chicago Press, 1968: 106-114.

18. Bennett M. Berger, "How Long is a Generation?" in *Looking for America.* Englewood Cliffs, N.J.: Prentice-Hall, 1971.

19. Ibid., p. 28.

20. Talcott Parsons and Gerald M. Platt, "Higher Education and Changing Socialization," in Matilda White Riley, Marylin Johnson, and Anne Foner, *Aging and Society: A Sociology of Age Stratification,* Vol. 3. New York: Russell Sage, 1972.

21. Leo W. Simmons, *The Role of the Aged in Primitive Societies.* New Haven, Conn.: Yale University Press, 1945.

22. Irving Rosow, "Old Age: One Moral Dilemma of an Affluent Society," op. cit.

23. We are not here providing the complete argument by Rosow but loosely relying upon it to show the effect of changes of societal structure upon the elders.

24. For a theory of aging based on degree of modernization of various societies, see *Aging and Modernization,* Donald Cowgill and Lowell Holmes, eds. New York: Appleton-Century-Crofts, 1972.

25. Emile Durkheim, *The Division of Labor in Society.* New York: Free Press, 1964.

26. H. H. Gerth and C. Wright Mills, from *Max Weber: Essays in Sociology.* New York: Oxford University Press, 1964.

27. Governmental assumption of responsibility for income for retired individuals began with the Social Security Act of 1935.

28. See the Introduction.

29. See M. Riley and A. Foner, *Aging and Society: An Inventory of Research Findings,* Vol. 1, New York: Russell Sage, 1968, for detailed data of labor-force participation by the elders. For example, the rate of participation by American males has followed this pattern:

Year:	1900	1940	1960	1975 (projected)
Age 20-24:	91.7	96.1	88.9	86.7
Age 65+:	9.1	7.4	10.5	9.8

30. In 1972 the median income for families with 65+ heads was $5,968 versus $11,870 for those with heads under 65. In 1972 the percentage of families under the poverty line ($2,505 for a family of two) was 9.3 percent for all ages and 11.6 percent for the over 65. The percentage is much higher for unrelated individuals: for all ages, males 29 percent and females 34.3 percent, for 65+ it is 37.1 percent for males and 40.4 percent for females ($1,994 being the poverty line). These figures gain further significance if we consider that in 1970 there were 138.5 women over 65 for each 100 men over 65. Data from DHEW, Adm. on Aging, publications No. (OHD) 74–20008 and (OHD/AOA) 72–20005.

31. See for example Erdman Palmore and Kenneth Manton, "Ageism Compared to Racism and Sexism," *Journal of Gerontology* 28 (1973): 363-369. The more important finding of this study is that indeed there is a discriminatory process against the aged, and that age produces more income inequality than race. Also see Raphael Ginzberg, "The Negative Attitude Toward the Elderly," *Geriatrics* 7 (1952): 297-302, for an account of the moral damage caused to the elders by the widespread negative feeling that they are a lost cause.

32. Irving Rosow, *Socialization to Old Age,* op. cit.

33. See Ralph Nader's study *Old Age: The Last Segregation.* Claire Townsend, Project Director, New York: Bantam, 1970, for a comparison between the proactive approach to care of the elders and the attempt to keep them outside of institutions in England, Denmark, and Sweden, and the reactive approach in this country which places stress on institutionalization.

34. See Charles H. Percy, *Growing Old in the Country of the Young,* New York: McGraw-Hill, 1974, for some interesting accounts of the plight of the elders by a member of the Senate's Special Committee on Aging.

35. See Sharon Curtin, *Nobody Ever Died of Old Age,* Boston: Little, Brown, 1972, for some vivid, although romanticized, portraits of poor elders.

36. Helena Znaniecki Lopata, *Widowhood in an American City,* Cambridge, Mass.: Schenkman, 1973, especially "Death of the Husband," pp. 47-50.

37. See Chapter 6 of this work, on nursing homes.

38. "By 'cultural dope' I refer to the man-in-the-sociologist's-society who produces the stable features of the society by acting in compliance with pre-established and legitimate alternatives of action that the common culture provides." In Harold Garfinkel, *Studies in Ethnomethodology.* Englewood Cliffs, N.J.: Prentice-Hall, 1967.

Also see Jacob Tuckman and Irving Lorge, " 'When Aging Begins' and Stereotypes about Aging," *Journal of Gerontology* 8 (1953): 489-491, for data finding that individuals who subscribe to the notion of aging as chronologically determined also are more likely to subscribe to stereotypes about the aged.

39. See an interesting, if fictional, account in the movie *Wild in the Street,* in which a very young and "hip" congresswoman tells the much older members of the

house that the greatest lesson America taught us is the importance of youth and that being old is "such a drag," and suggests lowering the required age for senators and presidents of the United States to 14 years of age.

40. See Chapter 4 of this work and Irving Rosow, *Social Integration of the Aged.* New York: Free Press, 1967.

41. See Chapter 4 of this work. Also see Zena Smith Blau, "Changes in Status and Age Identification," *American Sociological Review* 21 (1956): 198-203; and Jacob Tuckman and Irving Lorge, "Classification of the Self as Young, Middle-Aged, or Old," *Geriatrics* 9 (1954): 534-536. Tuckman and Lorge found that before the subjects of their study would classify themselves as old, their chronological age was quite high. For instance:

Chronological Age in Years	Classification as Old (%)
20-34	0
30-34	0
40-44	0
50-54	0
60-69	17
70-79	38
80 and over	53

42. Lewis Carroll, *Alice's Adventures in Wonderland.* New York: Signet Classics, 1960.

43. For a theoretical discussion of our point, see Alfred Schutz, "On Multiple Realities," in A. Schutz, *Collected Papers* I. The Hague: Martinus Nijhoff, 1971. The older individuals who isolate themselves are in a way collapsing two different realities into one: the world of their dreams and their paramount reality which become one with careful manipulation of individuals and settings surrounding them.

On the other hand, we are well aware of the problems of dispersing elders in the community at large; the point that proximity is equivalent to making friends has been proven wrong by Irving Rosow, *Social Integration of the Aged,* op. cit. Edward Hall makes the same point in *The Hidden Dimension,* Garden City, N.Y.: Anchor, 1966, in speaking about spacial relation among the English.

Chapter 3

THE MEANING OF LEISURE

Know that we have divided
In three our kingdom: and 'tis our fast interest
To shake all cares and business from our age;
Conferring them on younger strengths, while we
Unburden'd crawl toward death.[1]

In order to be able to proceed with an examination of how the older members of our society meaningfully employ their time free from work, which they by now possess in abundance,[2] we must try to understand what leisure is.

Many commonsensical notions of leisure run through the sociological and gerontological literature. Works purporting to weigh the successful adjustments to the later years of our life do not stop for a minute to define what leisure is.[3] Rather, they plunge headlong into showing what kind of activities older people engage in, with the implied assumption that leisure is activities and that successful retirement in the leisure years consists of participating in as many activities as possible.[4] What results is a culturally and chronologically biased notion of what successful aging is.

Students of leisure have not limited their programmatic approach to leisure activities to the elders alone, but have been generous with their advice to the population at large. This approach to leisure can be called a "popular-culture" approach.

It stems from the intellectual bias that "high culture" is what we should seek, and that the masses should be educated to enjoy good books, classical music, theaters, and the like, rather than fritter away their time watching television or a football game, or by gathering material possessions about them. David Riesman is a spokesman for this viewpoint. To wit: "Americans . . . go on a buying spree and end up possessed by their possessions—nostalgically still hungering after a vanished good life after the manner of Gatsby in Fitzgerald's novel."[5] And again: "As many thoughtful people have recognized our society offers little in the way of re-education for those who have been . . . exposed to all the blandishments of mass culture."[6]

Riesman is not alone in this view but is strongly backed by others such as MacIver, who gloomily states that while leisure is at our disposal, we lack the skills to enjoy it.[7] On the other side of the Atlantic, Riesman is echoed by the French scholar of leisure, Dumazedier.

Dumazedier, in his excellent work on French leisure,[8] passes judgment on the taste of the French populace to the point of assessing what constitutes "good movies" for them to see.

A second approach to leisure takes a dimmer view of the Pygmalion-like qualities of human beings, thus limiting itself to enumerating and spelling out the kinds of leisure activities in which various groups engage.[9] This approach provides us with data on activities but does not by itself tell us much about the sociological relevance of leisure.

Thus the parochial bias with which we view leisure mars our attempts to understand the cultural importance of it. We also possess a strong chronological bias when we speak of leisure for the elders. Chronological, since we as social scientists, policy makers, etc., often are not retired and elderly ourselves. Nevertheless, we take a privileged stance toward the elders and without consulting them we claim to "know" what older individuals ought or ought not to do to be successful.

Before proceeding to examine the literature dealing with the elders and their activities in their later years, we must provide a general picture of the possible meanings of leisure, thus avoiding the pitfall of a ready-made definition. We will not attempt a review of the whole field of leisure since it would be well beyond our scope.[10] However, our purpose here is to review three basic notions of leisure which implicitly or explicitly undergird much of the literature. We will show some of the ways in which these notions have been used and their implications for leisure. We then plan to offer a view of leisure which integrates the other views in a workable approach, thus enabling us to examine leisure for any group in our society, in our case the elderly.

Work Ethic

The dominant notion of leisure in the Western world places leisure at the polar opposite of work. We must go back a few centuries to see the seeds of the changing ideas of work that were to profoundly shape the destiny of Western man to our day. The great German sociologist Max Weber provided the key that opened the doors to the modern meaning of work and leisure.[11]

Weber was interested in studying social change. He focused on the phenomenon of capitalism and sought to see why it occurred only in certain cultures and in certain historical times. Weber was successful in his quest to disenchant the world and strip away the ideologies and myths which envelop our lives in a thick mist of taken-for-grantedness. In that respect he was not unlike Dorothy in *The Wizard of Oz* when she lifted the curtains that hid the props that allowed the wizard to legitimate his magic performance.

Weber was able to brush aside the rather naive explanations offered by other students of capitalism. Geographical determinants and claims of greediness as causes were dismissed by Weber, as well as the evolutional notion offered by Marx. It was this stern Teutonic sociologist who uncovered the source of capitalistic ideals: the religious ideals of Calvin and his followers.

In examining the notion of work held by Christianity before the religious upheaval brought about by Luther and Calvin, one is faced with the vision of toiling individuals copiously sweating from their brows to cleanse themselves of the original sin. After all, Adam and Eve had to engage in no labor in order to reap the plentiful fruits of the garden of Eden. When the two fell in disgrace, God condemned them to have to engage in physical labor in order to enjoy the fruits of this earth: "Therefore the Lord God sent him forth from the garden of Eden, to till the ground from whence he was taken."[1][2] There is, at this stage, nothing glorious about work itself: It is a burdensome task which must be fulfilled. However, if we want to come close to God the way is not through work but through meditation, as this is the way our spirit reaches communion with the Almighty. Thus, individuals seeking to be in touch with God retreated from worldly affairs into convents and monasteries giving birth to a large number of orders of nuns and monks.[1][3]

Luther brought a radical change to the meaning of work in the Christian world. Man had a "calling" to God in this world, and this "calling" could well be one's occupation. It mattered not, for Luther, whether one engaged in toiling the fields or baking bread in the cities; it was man's duty to do the best he could in his job to please God.

Calvin added the notion of predestination to Luther's theories. For Calvin and his followers God was an all-perfect, all-knowing, and all-powerful being. Thus God had already decided on the future course of human kind, sealing man's fate a priori. Man no longer could exercise a choice in regard to his future. A saintly, ascetic life was no longer a guarantee of heavenly bliss, following one's "calling" to God no longer led to salvation. God had already decided for us whether we would be saved or damned.

Calvinistic man found himself waiting for the inevitable to occur, without really knowing what to do while waiting. Man has, at different times, found himself in the anomic situation of biding time when the meaning of his doing and being were extremely unclear. Man's reaction has at times tended to be an amoral one; man has turned the confusion of the situation to his own advantage by equating lack of clear meaning with lack of scruples.[14] Another reaction has been the rather extreme one of taking one's life in the face of a loss of meaning.[15] A third reaction, commonly depicted in literary works[16] portrays man in futile abandonment when confronted with the void of meaningless existence.

But Calvinists were a far cry from the pathetic figures of Vladimir and Estragon in Beckett's play.[17] Calvinists refused to lie down and passively accept their fate. Although powerless to change destiny, man could seek signs of God's favor on this earth. Since God was a perfect being, thus reasoned man according to Weber, He would not deceive him, hence if He allowed man to be successful in his terrestrial endeavors He must be showing signs of His favor. Consequently, the more favors God granted man the more likely it would seem that the favored individual would be one of the chosen ones.

Success in one's endeavors became a way to seek signs of God's favor. This freed man from being bound to his original job, instead it became his duty to move on to better jobs thus continually seeking signs of celestial favor. Financial success became a way to win God's approval: "Remember, that *time* is money . . . remember that *credit* is money. . . . The more there is of it, [money] the more it produces every turning, so that the profits rise quicker and quicker."[18] But success was the key word not money. The followers of Calvin carried on their frugal and God-fearing existence while the material fruits of their success were reinvested in ways to lead to further success. The Calvinistic principles had led to the unanticipated consequence of a phenomenon that was to become known as capitalism.

Work was no longer a burden to be grimly carried but the very tool with which one sought God. Work had suddenly moved center stage and assumed primary importance. While the religious overtones which gave impetus to the process to ennoble work and to transform it from a vile necessity into the central meaning of life were slowly to be eroded away over the centuries, the idea that work was the very stuff of life continued very strongly to our days, no longer a Protestant ethic, but still a powerful work ethic.

Work and Leisure

Work is but a facet of man's life but this facet became very important to man. Individual lives took shape in terms of work as man's life cycle began being seen in terms of years preparatory to work, work-years, and retirement.[19] In our daily life we also divide time into work time and time off from work.[20] Man's conception of self-esteem and others' conception of him were seen largely in terms of his work. Man's work tended also to determine his social position, circle of friends, pursuits, interests, etc.

Sociologists began to study man in terms of his work. Everett Hughes led the way with *Men and Their Work.* Hughes' comment that no line of work can be understood outside the social matrix in which it occurs[21] was taken seriously by his fellow sociologists and studies of men in their professional settings became important in discussions about our society.[22] Man's striving to improve his life-position through improving his work situation[23] became crucial to the understanding of man. Individual behavior began to be seen as shaped by one's occupational position, to the point that one's voting behavior could be influenced by one's class position[24] or that one's sociocultural classification as young or old would be dependent upon one's occupational group.[25]

In short, Work with a capital W became the paramount element of our public social life, shaping it and reaching beyond it into our private lives and shaping them too. What about leisure? Dejected and forgotten, leisure took a back seat to work: "Leisure—even for those who do not work—is down at the bottom a function of work, flows from work, and changes as the nature of work changes."[26]

One spoke uneasily of leisure and leisure time as if the very mention of it possessed a negative connotation in a work-oriented society. Usually when we found out things about leisure it was through work. Man's occupation determined the leisure pursuits he engaged in.

Leisure tended to be seen in such a negative fashion that even its definitions were negative: the time which was not work.[27]

Other definitions were more specific: Leisure was the time which is not work and not needed for subsistance (eating, sleeping, etc.).[28] A more comprehensive definition still sees leisure as a series of nots: the time which is not work, the time which is not work-related (travelling to and from work and the like), the time which is not needed for physiological sustainment, the time which is not needed to engage in obligations partly related to one's work (having one's boss over for dinner), the time which is not any of these is discretionary time, time at our disposition, leisure time.[29]

But this is not to say that discretionary time is ours for the taking and can be freely utilized. Our occupation shapes how we will use this time. Wilensky[30] offers two possibilities of how work will shape our leisure time. Leisure time can be used for compensatory activities which will provide a surrogate for the needs which are not provided for by our principal activity: work. Thus, if we are assembly-line workers who engage in noncreative work performed in solitude we probably will seek creative leisure activities in the company of others.[31] On the other hand, leisure may be a spillover of our skills and interests from the work setting. Thus, if we are college professors, we will be likely to listen to "high-brow" classical music and go to theaters more often than a less "intellectual" group such as dentists.[32] We could even end up with a combination of compensatory and spillover activities as we may decide to go fishing to "blow off steam" and relieve work strain but we also engage in do-it-yourself activities which rely on our manual dexterity, carried over from work, as Gerstl shows us to be the case with dentists.[33]

But regardless of whether one "compensates" or "spills over," one seems to do so from work to leisure. Leisure seen in this way is literally no fun at all. It is a far cry from an existential choice of meaningful endeavors, from the freest time of our life. The work ethic has reduced leisure to that which we do while waiting to go back to work; we recuperate from a hard (but of course meaningful) day at the office or we relax to regenerate ourselves for tomorrow's workday.

The ramifications of work being preferred over leisure extend even deeper, pervading our whole life. Philip Slater[34] cries out in anguish against the effects of our way of life upon ourselves. While he is not speaking directly about work and leisure, it is clear that our goals strongly affect our work habits and our leisure pursuits. According to Slater, the extreme stress of competition and individualism in our lives leads to a paradoxical uniformity, as we seek to emulate our betters, thus largely cancelling out individuality in our vain quest to outdo others. Uniformity is thus unwittingly chosen by Americans, according to Slater, in their very claim to individuality and success, leaving us in the end with a long depressing line of men in grey flannel suits (or according to the whims of the fashion in checkered pants and red sport coats).

In this quest for individuality we flee to suburbia, where in our plastic tiled, freshly painted tract home we are lords of our private castle. We thus impose upon ourselves restrictions in our lifestyle by isolating ourselves and limiting our accessibility to friends and entertainment centers such as cinemas, theaters, etc. Another consequence of our quest for loneliness, according to Slater, is the do-it-yourself movement, which rather than being explained here as a spillover or compensatory activity is seen as an attempt to maintain privacy and a reluctance to engage in interpersonal relations with artisans and the like. Slater thus points out how our quest for loneliness profoundly affects many facets of our life including our leisure habits.

Margaret Mead looks at another change in our life-style brought about by the changes in our society.[35] As changes have occurred in our society due to automation, earning power, inflation, rising standard of living, etc., the relation between work and its worth has changed. Consequently, according to Mead, Americans have shifted their focus from work to the family: "Jobs are selected as they will bear on the home."[36] Work must adapt itself to the family, thus leaving the center stage to the family and taking a supporting role.

Robert Dubin's study of industrial workers bears out Margaret Mead's suggestion,[37] as it finds a definite shift away from work as a central life interest. Louis Orzack, on the other hand, qualifies Dubin's and Mead's work by pointing out that central life interest varies with different occupations, and work is more important for professionals than for industrial workers.

Swados, in his somewhat dated but still unique study[38] shows that work has not quite given up center stage to the family or to leisure for that matter. The rubber workers of Akron when confronted with a shorter work day overwhelmingly chose to sacrifice their leisure time to earn more money. Moonlighting became a popular way to spend one's free time thus gaining more money but less time to enjoy it.

S. M. Lipset and his associates in their classic work on the International Typesetters Union[39] furnish information on group association in off-work activities and its derivation from work. The typesetters, given the particularly skilled nature of their work, feel their work status to be above that accorded them by society but they are largely unable to associate with what they feel to be individuals of comparable status. At the same time, the typesetters are unwilling to associate with individuals who society sees as their equals but who they consider of inferior status. This difference between perceived and accorded status of work leads the typesetters to become rather clannish; they associate with other typesetters off duty, in their leisure hours.

Lipset's finding provides a powerful disclaimer to the notion of leisure as free, discretionary time, while it shows how other social factors affect it. What Hughes said about work,[40] that it must be considered in its larger social matrix, seems also to apply to leisure.

Leisure and Work

Lipset, Swados, Mead, Slater and others do not address leisure directly. They address work and we have to learn about leisure by seeing beyond work, to its consequences upon leisure. Other individuals consider leisure directly, albeit still juxtaposing it to work. Leisure is still seen very strongly in terms of the work ethic, thus suggestions for improving leisure are really aimed at improving work. Recuperative and relaxing endeavors will rejuvenate our body so that we shall face the "true" task to which we are appointed: work.

This group of individuals comprises a large number of writers who take the opportunity to provide us with insights on how we should best spend our time off to be properly recharged when work time resumes. This kind of advice ranges from the magical juggling of hours in order to rearrange the work week in various fashions: four days on—three days off, seven days on—seven days off, all the way to Pearson's radical suggestion[4 1] of the eight-day week (one would work for ten hours a day for four days and then have four days off). According to Pearson we would stagger the work force so that one-eighth of it would begin work on any given day, the next eighth the next day and so forth. We would in such a manner, according to Pearson, solve pressing problems of traffic congestion thus reducing our travel time to and from work as well as being presented with a golden chunk of four days off. Of course, given the scattered work schedules, we would have to choose our friends among those on similar schedules, and since only one-eighth of the work force has a schedule identical to ours, the pickings would be pretty slim.

The monograph *Leisure in America: Blessing or Curse?*[4 2] reflects the general work-ethic attitude toward leisure, especially in the article by its editor, James C. Charlesworth. Charlesworth realizes the complexity of our leisure problem. He duly notices that the Protestant ethic affects leisure potentials, that the upper-middle classes are concerned with competing with the Jones, that automation alienates people from their jobs, and even that the race with the Russians (to show that we are better than the Communists) puts the emphasis on productivity rather than on leisure.

Unfortunately, in his zeal to win the race with the USSR, Charlesworth suggests a somewhat dictatorial program of his own. Leisure, our beloved discretionary time, our free time, should according to Charlesworth, be administered by a state department of leisure, and "the government should take the prime responsibility for the wise use of leisure."[43] Further-more: "Leisure activities, mental and physical, should be com-pulsorily learned."[44] This learning, of course, is done for the good of the masses since: "Most people do not know what they want when it comes to developing their intellects, their person-alities, and their bodies."[45]

After Charlesworth, we found the view from the "opposite side," Boris Grushin's *Problems of Free Time in the U.S.S.R.,*[46] rather mild by comparison. In the USSR leisure is seen as a recuperative activity to better prepare workers to be fit to pro-duce for the nation. It is, however, one's duty to better oneself in his discretionary time. Of course the leading leisure activities in which the Soviet citizens engage take a predictable turn: Number one goes to participation in social work followed by political education while way down at the bottom of the list we find somewhat dubious leisure activities, according to Grushin, such as number 29 (religious devotion), and last on the list, number 30 (idling).[47]

We learn, in Grushin's work, that: "Marx said that under communism society's wealth would be gauged by free, rather than working time."[48] Thus, on January 1, 1968, all Soviet factories reduced working hours to a five-day, forty-one-hour week. The Russian citizens, however, still seem to be plagued by a lack of leisure time. Activities such as travelling to and from work and household chores seem to cut heavily into it. To solve this problem,

the drive for more free time should be waged today not against working time but against time off work, namely against those of its elements which require the expenditure of considerable effort without contribution to the development of personality.[49]

Naturally, current practices of gaining free time by paying less attention to one's children or placing a heavier load on housewives is not recommendable. Instead, reduction of travel-ling hours and the purchase of modern kitchen appliances may be a useful way of solving the problem, according to Grushin.

The quality of leisure is also important, thus it should be used to better the crowds, to develop their personalities. Grushin provides a Soviet brand of the "popular culture" approach to leisure,[50] but he is well aware that in the Western world popular culture implies the existence of an elite to guide the masses along the right path, and this somewhat contradicts Russian ideals. Thus, with an interesting twist, Grushin states that society should not concern itself with providing a cultural elite but with allowing individuals to share the genius of already existing cultural giants such as Leo Tolstoi.[51] Grushin does not concern himself with who will carry on the culture in the USSR, perhaps in his confidence in the immortal meaning of past Russian masters he does not feel the need of new cultural guidance.

The viewpoint of the importance of work, the paragon of the work ethic, is furnished by an early twentieth-century American sociologist, Thorstein Veblen. With ironic and biting prose Veblen attacks a particular class at a specific time of American history: the nouveaux riches, the Vanderbilts, the Harrimans, the Goulds, etc.[52] But Veblen's disdain for conspicuous consumption and leisure in the end proves an indictment of all who do not live by the sanctity of work but rather engage in what Veblen saw as useless pursuits. In the face of Veblen's attack leisure paled to a ghostly figure which barely appeared in the cracks flawing the powerful monolith of work.

For Veblen mere possession of wealth and power does not constitute enough ground for gaining esteem. Wealth must be displayed to provide evidence leading to the enhancement of esteem in the eyes of others. There are two ways to achieve this task: conspicuous leisure and conspicuous consumption. The former relies upon public displays showing that one can abstain from work and engage in a life of idleness. The latter complements the former. One cannot spend one's whole life in a public showcase and must surround oneself with markers of one's wealth by engaging in the conspicuous consumption of valuable goods.

Veblen scoffs at this squandering of time and money:

From the foregoing survey of the growth of conspicuous leisure and consumption, it appears that the utility of both alike for the purposes of reputability lies in the element of waste that is common to both. In the one case it is a waste of time and effort, in the other it is a waste of goods.[53]

Under the bite of Veblen's pen not only does leisure shrivel to a wasteful pursuit but other dearly-held elements of our daily life suddenly become repugnant. Take, for instance, one element that, according to Veblen, we use to prove our superior status: the dog. To wit:

The dog has advantages in the way of uselessness as well as in special gifts of temperament. He is often spoken of, in an eminent sense, as the friend of man, and his intelligence and his fidelity are praised. The meaning of this is that the dog is man's servant and that he has the gift of an unquestioning subservience and a slave's quickness in guessing his master's mood. Coupled with these traits . . . the dog has some characteristics which are of a more equivocal aesthetic value. He is the filthiest of the domestic animals in his person and the nastiest in his habits. For this he makes up in a servile, fawning attitude toward his master and a readiness to inflict damage and discomfort on all else.[54]

Clearly beagles like Snoopy lose some of their lovable nature when seen through Veblen's eyes. Veblen does not stop at our domestic animals and servants but irreverently assails more sacred elements of our life:

Priestly vestments show, in accentuated form, all the features that have been shown to be evidence of a servile status and a vicarious life. Even more strikingly than the everyday habit of the priest, the vestments, properly so called, are ornate, grotesque, inconvenient, and, at least ostensibly comfortless to the point of distress. The priest is at the same time expected to refrain from useful effort and, when before the public eye, to present an impassively disconsolate countenance, very much after the manner of a well-trained domestic servant.[55]

While Weber quoted Benjamin Franklin[56] to show the worth of time and work, Veblen bares the other face of the coin, the waste of not employing one's time usefully.

Leisure before Work

Some European scholars place a much more direct emphasis on leisure itself. They are, nevertheless, still deeply steeped in the work ethic. Kenneth Roberts belongs to this group.[57] Roberts defines leisure as what it is not, the time and the activities which are nonobligatory.

Leisure is still tied to work since all (in England) observe a common rhythm of life: work-time, holidays, evenings at home, etc. The large organizations which cater to leisure are geared to this rhythm, thus providing leisure opportunities at given times. Roberts, however, makes it clear that he feels that leisure has compartmentalized itself off from the influence of work. The reasons for this happening are to be found in the wide dispersion of popular leisure activities across class and occupational barriers. Growing alienation from work also causes people to look elsewhere to find meaning in their life. According to Roberts, people work in order to be able to do interesting things in their leisure time.

Roberts points out that there are factors which affect leisure much more than work. He notices that the division in styles of leisure are much sharper across age lines than across social class and sex lines.[58] He also lists some of the factors which seem to influence leisure in a more direct way than work: the style of family life (for instance, becoming a parent reduces the amount of free time), the community in which the individual lives (for instance, going to the local public house with your friends) and the professional organizations which cater leisure to the masses (since in their effort to reach as many people as possible they seek a common denominator of leisure).

Roberts' approach provides some interesting leads in the study of leisure by expanding the horizon of this concept and examining a larger social matrix of elements influencing leisure, rather than work alone.

The French sociologist Joffre Dumazedier also pulls drastically away from work as the main determinant of leisure activities. Dumazedier goes as far as stating that people move to certain locations and choose a certain job so as to be able to afford the kind of leisure they seek.[59] Dumazedier sees leisure as fulfilling three functions: *Relaxation* provides the individual with the chance to recover from the daily pressures, especially those stemming from work. *Entertainment* enables the individual to escape the daily routine which leads to boredom. Finally, *personal development* allows the individual to go beyond his schedule of daily concerns. He can improve his mind and body by engaging in nonutilitarian, creative activities.

Roberts and Dumazedier are beginning to show in their work that leisure can have merits of its own, without being the handmaiden of work,[60] their studies, however, still uphold the reciprocal influence of leisure and work.

Leisure over Work

We are done with the work ethic and ready to examine different conceptions of leisure. The next link in detaching leisure from work is to be found in a notion of leisure which stemmed in the Christian world before work emerged as the savior of man for the Protestants. This view, expressed by the German social philosopher Josef Pieper[61] can be better understood if one is familiar with the work-ethic ideals, thus we include it here after the onslaught of Weberian followers.

Pieper defends leisure but he does not reject work as something abominable, he simply points out that work and leisure live in different realms and shows how they are different.[62] Work-ethic ideals express a serious mistake, according to Pieper, in attempting to place every activity under the common denominator of work. They have gone to the extent of seeing all intellectual pursuits as work, thus placing a utilitarian notion upon all intellectual activities. By subscribing wholly to this ideal of work one would destroy the notion of pure academic learning by changing all learning into professional training.

Such a utilitarian ideal is also incorrect if we, as Pieper does, examine the ancient distinction between the two cognitive ways of knowing: *ratio* and *intellectus*. *Ratio* stands for the active process of knowing which is associated with work; *intellectus,* on the other hand, represents the receptive mode of the soul in its absorbing knowledge in a passive fashion and thus having nothing to do with work.

Work ideals became popular quite early; one of Plato's own companions (to think that Plato was an exponent of the classical view of leisure!),[63] Antisthenes, turned Hercules into the human ideal for he had performed super-human labors. Leisure quickly succumbed to such strength and became associated with idleness and sloth. Work became seen as an activity which fulfilled a social and functional purpose. What is more, man, in a work-ideals society became ready to suffer in vacuo, for no reason at all. Man came to mistrust anything which he could really enjoy only that which he had acquired toiling and working. This is, for Pieper, a misunderstanding of the Christian idea of sacrifice. Some of man's most sacred things, such as God's love to man and the Holy Spirit, were given to man as a free gift. In the beginning there is no work, in the beginning there is a gift.

Pieper says that leisure is mistakenly seen as sloth. The word *acedia* means indeed idleness but not sloth. Idleness in *acedia* signifies that man has renounced the claim implicit in his human dignity, thus refusing to be oneself in his existential despair.[64] Leisure, instead, is only possible in being at one with oneself; it is a mental and spiritual attitude. Leisure goes beyond the functional aspect of work. It is a nonactive entity; it is an inner contemplation, a calm that both allows man to grasp the meaning of the universe and to celebrate in his mind his being at one with the universe.

Leisure cannot be idleness, because idleness as existential despair is renouncing the world, while leisure makes us be at one with the world. Leisure thus becomes the human preserve of freedom, of education, and of culture since it provides man with the meaning of the world.

Pieper sees leisure in religious terms; he returns leisure to the pre-Protestant notion that it is through meditation that we reach unison with God. His is an extremely important notion of leisure in that it dissociates work from leisure while the two seemed inseparable under the work ethic. Pieper shows that the two are not comparable. One is an activity serving a social function while the other is a state of mind which worships God by recognizing the marvelous joys of the world in which we exist.

The Classical Notion of Leisure

Pieper's formulations point out that in staking so much on work we may have forgotten the true meaning of beauty unencumbered by utilitarian notions. The fine quality of Pieper's critique of the work ethic is largely lost in the wilderness as its whisper is drowned in the noise of a busy working world.

With Sebastian de Grazia it is a different story. De Grazia's masterful work[65] on leisure spans the centuries in a scholarly examination of work and leisure and dispels misconceptions about the two in a powerful and convincing fashion, which can not be ignored by friends or foes.

"Do you know what a holiday is?" asks de Grazia, and then provides the answer: "A day to dance in."[66] It is the same theme already played by Pieper, but our dancing here need not be to God, but to whatever we choose to dance about.

If we return to the classical notion of leisure, says de Grazia, we shall see that the Greek word *scholé* meant to have quiet or peace and to be able to do things for their own end. *Scholé* was freedom from having to labor. Work was seen as the negation of *scholé,* it was *ascholia.* In Latin, work was cast in a similarly negative fashion. Leisure was *otium,* while work became *negotium.*

In our modern world we have imprisoned ourselves in a clock-regulated schedule, giving up freedom to clocked time, says de Grazia. Thus, we have structured our lives in time periods, even changing a state of mind such as leisure into free time, a measurable entity. By so doing, we have changed a qualitative concept into a quantitative one. To wit:

> Work is the antonym of free time. But not of leisure. Leisure and free time live in different worlds. . . . Free time refers to a special way of calculating a special kind of time. Leisure refers to a state of being, a condition of man, which few desire and fewer achieve.[6 7]

Free time isn't free just because it is bound by a clocked time limit, thus, de Grazia points out, to speak of leisure time is a contradiction in terms, since leisure is a state of mind which cannot be constrained within time boundaries.

De Grazia launches an attack on the modern technological United States in the attempt to show how man's search for happiness is misguided. De Grazia does not call for educational or governmental[6 8] measures to educate the masses to pursue leisure. He claims clearly that only a few individuals are capable of and indeed want leisure.

What the rest of the people seek is not leisure but abundance:

> The Indians sold Manhattan for a few trinkets. It would seem they were not the only ones to be taken in by a handful of beads. Dazzled by the jugglers, the individual sold his time for shiny objects. We have seen him fall prey to advertising and turn into a consumer. The things he now wants cost money, money costs work, work costs time.[6 9]

De Grazia continues by showing how the mania for buying confines people to a vicious circle of consuming goods and busying themselves with activities. People are rushing so much that they never stop to look at themselves; they never confront their naked self.

Modern man has reversed the classical notion of the pursuit of happiness through leisure by making happiness possible only through work. Man has reversed the classical idea of not-working as a desirable state by placing a negative connotation on leisure: no longer is work *neg-otium* but leisure is *un-employment*. Modern man has regulated his life with clocks. After all this we still speak of leisure time! De Grazia asks: "Are democracy and leisure compatible?"[7 0] His answer is unequivocal:

"No. In democracy today free time does exist, though in less quantity than it is thought; of leisure, there is none."[71]

What then is leisure for de Grazia? His answer is that it does not matter *what* constitutes leisure but that anything can be leisure or work depending on the reason why it is done: It is leisure if it is chosen for its own sake. A man of leisure cannot work in the sense of having to make a living, his endeavors will always be play and not work. Life is a game for the man of leisure and all his activities will be plays of his mind, intellectual pursuits in their own right. Men of leisure, unconstrained by the shackles of necessity will "invent the stories, they create the cosmos, they discover what truth is given man to discover, and give him the best portion of truth and error."[72] With de Grazia, leisure has taken a privileged position while work has been reduced to little more than prostituting one's mind for tangible remuneration.

We have come the full circle, from work as the aegis of man's quest for happiness to work as the negation of man's true happiness. Leisure has risen to the limelight with a vengeance in de Grazia's words: Not only is it a superior state than work but it is a selected one, only for the few. The rest of us, the plodders, the uninspired, the consumers, keep buying and busying ourselves, keep imitating each other in our pursuit for more material possessions. In so doing we all come to look alike in a conforming circle of uniform, depersonalized pursuit of goods,[73] while we wander on pursuing the chimera of happiness:

Like the Indian following the buffalo, the American follows his job. . . . Already called by his first name by his new friends, brushing his teeth with the same toothpaste, in a home with the same refrigeration and heat, with Johnny and Bessie in school, and their mother in the PTA, finding the same supermarket and drugstore, the same movies coming out of Hollywood, and the same babysitter or her twin to sit in front of the TV while baby is sleeping, all the migrating working-man needs is a few vines growing in pots to make him feel he has taken roots.[74]

Leisure Freely Chosen

We have briefly surveyed various interpretations and explanations of leisure. If there has been a notable absence of figures
and tables informing us exactly of how many weekly hours of
leisure we may expect, what they consist of, and how to cope
with them, it was no accident. The point we intended to make
was that leisure is not clearly definable, categorizable, and
measurable. The problematic nature of leisure can be seen in
the varied and often contradictory ways in which various scholars have dealt with it.

Our review began by examining the Protestant ethic and its
modern followers, the advocates of the work ethic. After
leaving the work ethic with the scorching words of Veblen,
we examined Roberts and Dumazedier to show the increasing
importance of leisure in its own right, rather than as a mere
appendix of work. Next, Pieper and de Grazia pointed out
that we have been dealing with a skewed comparison in trying
to parallelize two different entities such as work and leisure.

We have seen Riesman's preoccupation with his fellow Americans, concerning their avidity for material possessions. Riesman
has hopes of redemption for them, hopes to which he, however,
refers only vaguely. From Riesman we went to de Grazia, who
is also preoccupied (or rather, disgusted) with modern Americans' hunger for abundance. However, he gloomily turns his
thumb down on the possibility that the populace may learn
how to appreciate leisure.

We have spanned from the extreme of Charlesworth and
Grushin to the extreme of de Grazia. Charlesworth seeks a
nation in which we can all appreciate leisure and he feels that
forcing it upon us will "teach" us how to enjoy leisure. Grushin
makes a strange bedfellow for the rather ethnocentric Charlesworth, but they belong in the same corner, since Grushin
also invokes a controlled notion of leisure (even providing a
list of desirable leisure activities). He also goes as far as negat-
ing the need for a cultural elite to show the way to others. De
Grazia would shudder at such a thought. Leisure cannot be con-

trolled, listed, or learned, he would claim, since the very notion of leisure is free choice of activities.

While we heartily agree with de Grazia that to speak of leisure and control of leisure in the same breath is a basic misunderstanding, we do not share de Grazia's strong intellectual bias. De Grazia is too negative when he states that there is no leisure in America today.

To be sure he has some reasons. Truly enough, if leisure is controlled by time, how can it be leisure in a pure sense? But what of a country in which we all work? Both Kenneth Roberts[75] and Bennett Berger[76] make the point that democracy has done away with a leisure class in the classical sense.[77] But the fact that we all work and are subject to the same rhythm of life does not deny us, as we see it, the possibility of enjoying a state of mind called leisure. Indeed, de Grazia's claim that a few individuals face life with a pure spirit of play and that they are the bearers of our culture, the discoverers of paths to tomorrow, is unsubstantiated. If we follow logically de Grazia's assumption that leisure is not possible in a democracy, we come up with a staggering conclusion: No new intellectual development is possible in the United States since there is no group completely devoted to leisure. But one has only to look at our development to see the absurdity of such a claim.

De Grazia is blinded by his parochial notion of what leisure is. After making strong claims to the effect that freedom of choice constitutes leisure, he wipes out with a series of deadly blows the activities in which Americans engage as possible leisure pursuits. But if leisure is a state of mind, any activity can be leisure in the proper state of mind.

We would like to point out that abundance need not be something different from leisure, that the two can be one and the same. If basking in the sun provides us with the spirit of leisure we find it commendable, but if we find the feeling of leisure in surrounding ourselves with material possessions, then this too is leisure. The key point is that we freely choose abundance in that we enjoy it, rather than choosing it "to keep up with the Joneses."

When Riesman sadly comments that Americans lust for the way of life of Jay Gatsby,[78] he, alone with de Grazia, fails to see that aesthetic pleasures and leisurely pursuits can be found in more than one way. Consider the following:

> He had been projected into another chamber and was sitting in a sunken bath with his head just above the level of the floor. All about him, lining the walls of the room and the sides and bottom of the bath itself, was a blue aquarium, and gazing through the crystal surface on which he sat, he could see fish swimming among amber lights and even gliding without curiosity past his outstretched toes, which were separated from them only by the thickness of the crystal. From overhead, sunlight came down through sea-green glass. 'I suppose, sir, that you'd like hot rosewater and soapsuds this morning, sir—and perhaps cold salt water to finish.'[79]

The quality and tone of the above description certainly turns a morning bath from a routine ablution into a leisure pursuit.

De Grazia limits his attack on consumerism to the gross features of it ignoring its finer possibilities. But even if we consider the "gross" features, what may seem repulsive to us may be someone else's leisure. For instance, riding a motorbike on a dusty, brown trail may elicit in us a feeling of summer flies, of annoyance. For others, that bike may be a modern-day stallion, a wildfire with which to conquer what is left of the Old West, the desert dunes.

Leisure Today

Our discussion of de Grazia and our defense of abundance was meant to point out that if we consider leisure as freely chosen pursuits, we should not limit that choice to our taste or intellectual appreciation. If de Grazia is intellectually biased, if the work ethic misunderstands leisure, what are we left with?

Let us review our situation today. Organizational and technological development in our society have changed the ideological justifications that make our everyday life possible. One of these changes, concerning our work ethic, began showing itself with the advent of industrialization whereby work became more impersonal and routinized. Our society failed to provide the appropriate ideology to ennoble the jobs that the new system required, thus alienating people from their jobs, and weakening the work ethic. People began considering their work just a job. Time off from work became free time, thus underscoring the burdensome nature of work.

The organization and distribution of labor was instrumental in the decline of the work ethic. There was an evergrowing shift from small to large businesses. The corporate channels of mobility changed drastically, as people went to work for large corporations rather than being self-employed.

Another important factor in the decline of the work ethic was the rising income in a postindustrial society. As more people became part of the service force, less and less were needed to produce goods. Increasing numbers of individuals committed themselves to occupations whose viability depended on a higher level of affluence, travel agents, therapists, etc. Sociability became more important than achievement; individuals began looking at life in terms of "getting along" rather than "getting ahead."[80]

The work ethic, however, refused to die. It still lingers in all of us and makes us somehow feel uneasy about our newly acquired opulence. We feel guilty about doing nothing. We have all become, in Berger's words, "compromised Greek citizens carrying the burden of compromised Protestant ethics."[81]
The notion of work orientation has been replaced by one of activity orientation. As work may no longer be ennobling in itself, we are left with the notion of doing, being active. It matters not what we do, it is the doing in itself that matters. Activity now possesses the positive connotation once associated with work, while being passive is still largely seen in negative terms (we justify our moments of passive behavior, for example, we do not simply lie in the sun, but we are "suntanning," or we do not simply lie on the grass, but "go on a picnic," etc.).

This is where we are today, no longer forcefully driven by the work ethic, but not quite comfortable without it. Thus, in examining the leisure of any group in our society we must be careful not to oversimplify the meaning of leisure in the temptation of obtaining clear-cut results to our inquiries. Approaching sociological concepts as "paired concepts"[82] has been shown not to reflect the ambiguity that exists in the social world. It would be nice to be able to dichotomize concepts in sociology: "socialization and individualization, primary and secondary relations, status and contract, symbiosis and co-operation, Gemeinschaft and Gesellschaft,"[83] and we may add: work and leisure.

What now faces us instead is an amorphous notion of leisure. However, we can find a common ground for leisure. Keeping in mind the various factors that influence leisure, such as work, the family, clocked time, etc., leisure in the end is what we choose to do purposefully in our discretionary time. Not all discretionary time is leisure. If what we do is dictated by social pressures to behave in certain ways or by the attempt to merely fill in some empty time, that is not leisure. If our self-fulfillment stems from purchasing a fashionable house in East Egg, or buying a pale yellow coupé, or obtaining the love of Daisy Buchanan,[84] that is leisure. If our self-fulfillment comes from gazing at the stars, that is leisure. If we just sit and ecstatically watch the river flow, then that too is leisure.

NOTES

1. William Shakespeare, *King Lear,* Act I, Scene I.

2. See "Employment and Retirement," by S. Wolfbein and E. Burgess in *Aging in Western Societies,* op. cit., for a review of data summarizing increases in life-expectancy, and the years spent outside the labor force.

3. Many works do not even consider leisure in examining adjustment to the older years of our lives. They simply speak of "activities" or "interactions" in which the elders do or should engage; see among others, E. Cumming and W. E. Henry, op. cit.

4. Max Kaplan, "The Uses of Leisure," in C. Tibbitts, op. cit. Kaplan examined activity level in relation to occupational level; his work is programmatic in calling for a high level of activity in old age. To aid the elders Kaplan envisions a new professional breed: leisure counselors.

5. R. Weiss and D. Riesman, "Some Issues in the Future of Leisure," in E. Smigel, ed., op. cit., p. 179.

6. D. Riesman, "Work and Leisure in Post-Industrial Society," *Mass Leisure,* E. Larrabee and R. Meyersohn, eds. Glencoe, Ill.: Free Press, 1960, p. 365.

7. R. McIver, *The Pursuit of Happiness.* New York: Simon and Schuster, 1955.

8. J. Dumazedier, *Toward a Society of Leisure.* London: Collier-Macmillan, 1962.

9. See, for instance, the article by C. Wright and H. Hyman, "Voluntary Association Memberships of American Adults," in Larrabee and Meyersohn, op. cit.

10. For a recent comprehensive review of the literature, see Stanley Parker, op. cit.

11. While an in-depth examination of Weber's work on religion is well beyond our scope, a cursory review of *The Protestant Ethic and the Spirit of Capitalism* is necessary to understand the modern-day Western notion of leisure.

12. *The Holy Bible,* King James' version, Genesis 23. New York: Cambridge University Press.

13. For an extensive background of leisure see the unsurpassed work of Sebastian de Grazia, op. cit.

14. See N. Machiavelli, *The Prince,* London: Oxford University Press, 1960; and F. Guicciardini, *The History of Italy and History of Florence,* New York: Twayne, 1964, for a review of amoral man in a meaningless situation.

15. See E. Durkheim, *Suicide,* New York: Free Press, 1951, especially anomic suicide, for such a view.

16. See, for instance, S. Beckett, *Waiting for Godot,* New York: Grove, 1954, which portrays the futility of man when waiting for God-ot, but not knowing why or what for.

17. Beckett, op. cit.

18. Benjamin Franklin in M. Weber, op. cit.

19. See, for instance, B. Neugarten and J. Moore, "The Changing Age-Status System," *Middle Age and Aging,* B. Neugarten, ed., op. cit.

20. E. Hughes, *Men and Their Work.* Glencoe, Ill.: Free Press, 1958.

21. E. Hughes, op. cit.

22. See, among others, M. Dalton's study of managerial positions in *Men Who Manage,* New York: John Wiley, 1959; and E. Freidson's examination of our most sacred profession: doctors, in *Profession of Medicine.* New York: Dodd, Mead, 1970.

23. See H. Wilensky, "The Professionalization of Everyone?" *The Sociology of Organizations,* O. Grusky and G. Miller, eds., for a social trend toward gaining more power and prestige by successfully changing one's occupational group in a profession.

24. M. Lipset, "Elections: The Expression of the Democratic Class Struggle," *Class, Status, and Power,* R. Bendix and S. M. Lipset, eds. New York: Free Press, 1966.

25. B. Berger, "How Long is a Generation?" *Looking for America,* op. cit.

26. C. Greenberg, "Work and Leisure under Industrialism," E. Larrabee and R. Meyersohn, op. cit.

27. See, for instance, G. A. Lundberg et al., *Leisure—A Suburban Study.* New York: Columbia University Press, 1934.

28. A. Giddens, "Notes on the Concept of Play and Leisure," *Sociological Review* 12 (1964): 73-89.

29. S. Parker, op. cit.

30. H. Wilensky, "Work, Careers and Social Integration," *International Social Science Journal* 12 (1960): 543-560.

31. Faunce in T. Kando and W. Summers, "The Impact of Work and Leisure," *Pacific Sociological Review* 14 (1971): 310-324.

32. J. Gerstl, "Leisure, Taste and Occupational Milieu," in E. Smigel, ed., op. cit.

33. J. Gerstl, in E. Smigel, op. cit.

34. P. Slater, *The Pursuit of Loneliness.* Boston: Beacon, 1970.

35. M. Mead, "The Pattern of Leisure in Contemporary America," Larrabee and Meyersohn, op. cit.

36. M. Mead, op. cit., p. 14.

37. R. Dubin, "Industrial Workers' World: A Study of the 'Central Life Interests' of Industrial Workers," in Smigel, op. cit.

38. H. Swados, "Less Work—Less Leisure," in Larrabee and Meyersohn, op. cit.

39. S. M. Lipset, J. Coleman and M. Trow, *Union Democracy.* Garden City, N.Y.: Anchor, 1956.

40. E. Hughes, op. cit.

41. See John W. Pearson, *The Eight Day Week,* New York: Harper & Row, 1973, for a summary of the different ways of changing our weekly work schedule.

42. J. Charlesworth, ed., *Leisure in America: Blessing or Curse?* Philadelphia: The American Academy of Political and Social Sciences, 1964.

43. Ibid., p. 36.

44. Ibid., p. 38.

45. Ibid., p. 41.

46. B. Grushin, *Problems of Free Time in the USSR,* A.N.H., 1969.

47. Ibid., pp. 9-10.

48. Ibid., p. 24.

49. Ibid., p. 38.

50. Grushin relies heavily on the work of Dumazedier, op. cit.

51. Grushin, op. cit., p. 84.

52. T. Veblen, *The Theory of the Leisure Class.* New York: Mentor Books, 1953.

53. T. Veblen, op. cit., p. 71.

54. Ibid., p. 103.

55. Ibid., p. 128.

56. Max Weber, op. cit.

57. Kenneth Roberts, *Leisure.* London: Longman, 1970.

58. Roberts' data was furnished by a BBC report on the number of hours English people watch television. See Roberts, op. cit.

59. Joffre Dumazedier, op. cit.

60. One cannot help but notice that the pull away from work is carried on by European scholars such as Roberts, Dumazedier, de Grazia, Pieper.

61. Josef Pieper, *Leisure the Basis of Culture.* New York: Pantheon, 1964.

62. Josef Pieper, op. cit.

63. S. de Grazia, op. cit.

64. See, for instance, the work of Søren Kierkegaard for a similar view of man. The Danish philosopher attacked the unreflective churchgoers, who lived through their lives without seeking the true meaning of being a Christian. See also Sebastian de Grazia, op. cit., for the notion of unreflective constant motion holding us back from taking a good look at ourselves.

65. De Grazia, op. cit.

66. Ibid., p. 7.

67. De Grazia, op. cit., p. 5.

68. Riesman, op. cit., and Charlesworth, op. cit.

69. De Grazia, op. cit., p. 334.

70. Ibid., p. 334.

71. Ibid., p. 334.

72. De Grazia, op. cit., p. 359.

73. For a similar viewpoint, see Slater, op. cit.

74. De Grazia, op. cit., p. 229.

75. Roberts, op. cit.

76. Berger in Smigel, op. cit.

77. See Clive Bell, "How to Make a Civilization," in Larrabee and Meyersohn, op. cit., for the opinion that we should return to having a leisure class in the classical sense, to preserve our civilization.

78. D. Riesman in Smigel, op. cit.

79. F. S. Fitzgerald, "The Diamond as Big as the Ritz," in *Babylon Revisited and Other Stories.* New York: Scribner's, 1960.

80. W. F. Whyte, Jr., *The Organization Man,* New York: Simon and Schuster, 1952; and D. Riesman, *The Lonely Crowd,* op. cit.

81. B. Berger in Smigel, op. cit., p. 27.

82. R. Bendix and B. Berger, "Images of Society and Problems of Concept Formation in Sociology," *Symposium on Sociological Theory,* Llewellyn Gross, ed. New York: Harper & Row, 1959.

83. Ibid., p. 98.

84. F. S. Fitzgerald, *The Great Gatsby.* New York: Scribner's, 1925.

Chapter 4

GROWING OLD GRACEFULLY

> *With mirth and laughter let old wrinkles come;*
> *And let my liver rather heat with wine*
> *Than my heart cool with mortifying groans.*[1]

Do individuals really merrily laugh, drink wine, roll up their trousers, slacken their belts, and sit under magnolia trees when they grow old? It is the purpose of this chapter to discover just that.

Living in Southern California proved to be a boon for such an enterprise, since although the migration west of American pioneers ended long ago, the westward push of old people has just begun.[2] Just far enough inland to avoid the coastal fog, just north enough to avoid the smog of the megalopolis, there lies a town which shall be named Hidden Valley. Hidden Valley is fairly small, comprising 55,000 inhabitants or thereabouts. The dry, warm climate of the area appeals to older people and 30 percent of the population is senior citizens; seniors referring to those individuals who have passed the chronological threshold of fifty.

The rolling hills surrounding Hidden Valley are covered with the luscious green of avocado groves, the greenery being broken here and there by the sunny color of oranges and tangerines. The greenery is also interrupted by a large number of vast mansions which form various residential communities or ranchos, as commonly called in this area.

It is in this town that I decided to set the stage for the research described in this chapter. The nature of Hidden Valley was ideal to a study of middle- and upper-class elderly citizens.[3] Chance also proved important in my selection. At the time I was teaching gerontology in a community college only five miles away, and many of the students in my classes were elders from Hidden Valley. This provided me with an excellent pool of possible research subjects and opened the doors for research in a variety of settings in the town.

One of these settings constitutes the nucleus around which this chapter revolves: the Corbett Senior Center. The center proved to be a useful source of inquiry for various reasons. As it will be shown later, the development of the center itself became an example of the struggle undertaken by a group of elderly to retain autonomy in the face of the spreading monolithic power of organized bureaucracy. The center offers the elders the possibility to engage in many organized leisure activities, thus enabling me to see what activities the elderly engaged or did not engage in, and to what extent they provided the impetus for organizing these activities. The center also became the location at which I met many of my subjects and conducted a large number of my interviews. Furthermore, through my contacts at the center I was able to visit some elders in their homes and observe their home life.

It is important to note that I was able to conduct my research in a setting in which the requirement for membership is that of advanced age: one has to be fifty[4] (I am in my early thirties) to enter the premises.

My entrée was greatly facilitated by the fact that the recreation coordinator of the center was a student in my gerontology classes and became a close personal friend. In fact, not only could I come and go as I pleased, but I had access to all of the files, and was able to use the coordinator's office and secretarial staff.

This chapter will then be focused around the center, in a twofold fashion. The brief history and troubled development of the center itself will be examined first; this will be followed by an examination of the elders, their different types, and the activities in which they engage.

The Setting

Come to our Luau on July 17th. Our Get Acquainted Party this month will be held at 1:30 p.m. and will be a potluck salad with an Hawaiian theme.

Dress in your mumus, wear flowers in your hair and if your last initial is A through P, please bring a salad or Q through Z, please bring a dessert.

I had spent a good part of the morning driving through the sunny streets of Hidden Valley looking for the center when finally I passed the right park and turned by the old trailer court and came upon it: an imposing golden-colored, Spanish-styled building surrounded by a closely clipped lawn and by the sparse shade of eucalyptus trees. Contrasting with the flowing arches of the center, behind it, almost suffocated by it, is a smallish, washed-out, wooden structure which used to be the original center.

Having passed the high, heavy wooden door, I was now faced by a large sign inviting all newcomers to a luau. After taking stock of whether I ought to bring a salad or a dessert, I stepped in and let my eyes wander around. The newness hits a newcomer at first, closely followed by the movement of people in and around the spacious inside. A large hall serves various functions; it is a passageway to the various smaller rooms in which the elders play cards, hold meetings, tap-dance, knit, etc. It also provides a resting place with a sofa and a few armchairs in which a few venerable oldsters sit and watch the passing of others or wait their turn to play pool in the next room. A coffee pot sits across the way, next to the long window beyond which is the office. There stay the volunteers, partitioned off from the rest of the elders. Further down the hall, through a double swinging door, is the large ballroom (or meeting room, according to the occasion); to the right of it is the small library towered by a large color television set.

This is the setting to which the seniors of Hidden Valley flock to in large numbers, about 11,000 seniors a month visit the place, to participate in leisure pursuits, to mill around, or just to get out from underfoot while their spouse cleans the house. By no means do they spend their whole day here; they come and go, one moment the place is swarming with white-haired grandmothers here for their weekly luncheon, the next minute everything is quiet, no one is here, apart from the "hard-core" group of twenty or thirty people who spend most of their days in the pool room or out by the shuffleboard courts.

Apart from its newness and large number of visitors, the center is not dissimilar from other centers in its purpose. It provides a series of services for senior citizens: legal help, blood pressure check-ups, bazaar sales of senior-made goods, etc.

What is different about the Corbett Senior Center is that it comes under the jurisdiction of the Parks and Recreation Department of Hidden Valley (while most centers are run by private concerns such as banks, the Salvation Army, etc.). This fact creates attrition between some elders and the recreation coordinator, who is a city employee in charge of activities at the center.

This attrition and the causes of it provide interesting data for the quest of this study towards understanding the meaning attributed by the elderly to their "golden years." Examining the center reveals that some elderly, even if a small minority, do not passively lie down and allow others to lead them. On the contrary, some elders keep the fight going, against insurmountable odds, and the fight itself becomes the meaning of their lives.

The Seven[5]

In 1960 a group of eight individuals, then in their sixties, decided to formalize their frequent encounters for leisure endeavors and formed a senior club. They met at each others' homes for about a year and played cards, had potluck dinners and from time to time, even dances. By the end of the year others had joined the club and their private residences became inadequate for the meetings.

A canvassing of the local churches provided some room for the club meetings, but it was merely a stopgap until a more permanent place could be found. At this time one of the original eight founders of the club died and left his small wooden house to be used as a club house. However, zoning laws prohibited such a use at the original location, and the seven founders of the club turned to the city administration's parks and recreation department for help. Help came. The small house was moved to a different location on city land, thus allowing for club meetings and relieving the club of tax and utilities expenditures.

Two things began to happen. First, what had originated as a small, informal get-together club was on its way to becoming a formal organization: A membership fee of one dollar was demanded and elections of officials were held. It mattered little that the original "seven" were the only ones running for office and that the president became the treasurer at the next elections, the dance chairman took over the presidency, and so on. Formal roles with formally prescribed and proscribed behaviors were now a part of the senior club. The second thing that happened was less felicitous for the "seven." What had begun as a club for seniors by seniors was quickly being taken over by the city. A city employee was placed in the club to "oversee the city property." In practice the employee answered the telephone and provided callers with information about the club.

By now the "seven" recognized the encroachment upon their turf. What had begun as a *home territory*[6] was being invaded by the city, which was beginning to change it into a *public territory:* no longer the private enclave of a group of friends but a public domain opened to all.

The invasion was not taken lightly or passively. The "seven" marched repeatedly on city hall carrying protest signs reading: "Get the City out of the Senior Club . . . Leave the Senior Club alone. . . ." But it was too late. The city, with its bureaucratic machine, had set its foot in by donating the land on which the club sat. Like a red dye rising from the ground, the bureaucracy was taking over the building and beginning to spread uncontrollably.

This problem is certainly not new. The German sociologist Georg Simmel recognized it as the crucial conflict in our modern society.[7] Individuals create an organizational form to serve them and before they know it, they are serving the organization. The problems of incorporating the elders within large organizations have been dealt with by others;[8] in this chapter the concern is not whether bridling an organization is possible or not, but the reaction of the individuals who are being supplanted by the growth of the organization.

The city decided it was time to hire a part-time coordinator, Mrs. Reed, to organize the activities of the club, and changed the name of the place from Senior Club to Hidden Valley Senior Center. The "seven" did not give up. They kept their club alive within the senior center, although they had the large handicap, among others, of having to charge a membership fee to provide some funds, while the senior center, backed by city money, offered free membership. The "seven" zeroed in on the tangible element of the usurpation by the city—Mrs. Reed—and they harassed and verbally abused the "intruder" to the point that she quit her job.

But the city did not quit. On the contrary, the parks and recreation department decided to place a full-time recreation coordinator in charge of the center. The individual chosen for the job was a young man in his thirties. He was a gentle soul who once had been a priest, but who, nevertheless, became a representative of city encroachment in the eyes of the "seven," and a young whippersnapper at that!

Young Joseph tried to run the center with the patience and understanding that had characterized his religious days. It did not work. The "seven" attacked him mercilessly: He would organize an afternoon dance only to be asked to leave until the dance was over (after all he was not a senior); he would attempt to institute a new policy only to have one of the "seven" telephone the mayor or more often beat on his door at city hall complaining that the new policy did not reflect the wishes of the elderly. Joseph's approach proved futile and he resigned in desperation.

At this time, the early seventies, the city applied for and received a federal grant to build a new senior center. The new coordinator chosen for the job was Mrs. Morgan, a senior herself, known and liked by the other seniors.

Mrs. Morgan took her position at the old center as work on the new one had just begun. Enthusiastic about her new job, the new coordinator did not at first realize the change that had taken place. She had been hired by the city and her claim to membership as a senior had been superceded by the one of the organization she now worked for, which made her the "enemy." Her first day at work provided her with a rude awakening. She rearranged the furniture in her office only to find it back in its original location after lunch.

Having realized the animosity of the "seven" toward her, she called a meeting with them and asked for their cooperation in running the center. The "seven" had hoped that the quitting of Joseph would discourage the city from further attempts at running the center, but their hopes were thwarted. Not only had a new coordinator been hired, but she was now attempting to change the decor of the place and even asking them to sanction her position by cooperating with her. They acrimoniously rejected her offer.

The struggle came to the surface. Until now the "seven" had been able to freely vent their frustrations about the encroachment of the city upon their club by zeroing in on the various coordinators. Joseph especially had been the ideal "flak-catcher"[9] ready to turn the other cheek when abused. Mrs. Morgan did not see her position as that of a "flak-catcher." She quickly used the powers bestowed upon her to control the situation. She began to plan and schedule events: classes in cooking, home repair, ancient history, creative writing, more trips for seniors, etc.

The "seven" attempted to undo the barrage of new changes

by appealing to the higher echelons of the city. They fought every change made by the coordinator; they called upon the director of parks and recreations, then upon the city manager, and finally upon the mayor, to no avail.

The "seven" then turned their frustration upon Mrs. Morgan. She would catch flak after all. Telephone calls in the middle of the night awoke Mrs. Morgan warning her of the terrible disasters that were occurring at the center. She drove to the center many times only to find it in dark stillness. Hate mail began reaching her desk and she was welcomed at the center by verbal abuse. Once sugar was slipped in the gas tank of her car, but Mrs. Morgan withstood the various crises and stayed on.

The new center was by now, 1974, ready. The claim to power by the "seven" became weaker. The city had set up an organization run by a coordinator who was herself a senior and by part-time workers and volunteers who were also seniors; the city owned the land and the building. Rules became tighter: no smoking in the building, no use of any rooms before receiving permission from the coordinator, no one in the building before 9:00 a.m. or after 4:00 p.m.

Ironically, the "seven" managed to retort by using the same tactics which the city had used. They donated $15,000 worth of furniture to the new center, overriding (for once) the protests of the coordinator. Thus, the ambiguous situation of territoriality which had begun with land versus building ownership was now continued in the form of building versus furniture.

Two years have passed, the "seven" have been fighting the coordinator to the yells of: "We paid for that desk, give us what we ask for or we shall take it back." But they have been losing ground. In 1974 when the new center was opened there were eight classes, 11 clubs and two services offered. The staff comprised the coordinator, two half-time office workers, and one custodian. Two years later, there are 43 clubs, 14 classes and 17 services offered. The staff includes the coordinator, a full-time assistant, eight office workers, a travel officer, and two custodians.

Seniors are slowly deserting the original Senior Club of the "seven." Whatever the club offers is also offered by the center on a larger scale. The center has a paid staff and the city's organizational and financial backing. The Senior Club still requires a membership fee while the center offers it free. Some individuals don't see any need to pay a dollar when they can have the same service at no cost. Others shy away from the Senior Club with claims such as: "We just want to enjoy ourselves, not fight."

Why do the "seven" continue their battle? When confronted with that question the "seven" tended to show visible signs of being upset. They feel that they have been instrumental in the creation of the center. They founded the original club that provided the impetus for the whole enterprise; they spread the word; they organized activities, sought new members, etc. In short, they gave their whole selves to the center, only to see the city take it away from them, to the point that they now can't even have a key to it.

When I asked questions about the past occupations of the "seven," I was met with vagueness and disinterest. They would rather talk about the happenings at the center today. Inquiries revealed that the "seven" had held rather low-prestige positions in their past lives. They had worked as secretaries, sales persons, or had been housewives. One of them had been a warrant officer in the navy and had been troubled by his inability to be a full-fledged officer, to the point that he had been heard saying: "I'd give my right arm to be an officer."

Having retired, they seemed to be headed toward the quiet and graceful way of aging typical of many elderly with no economic problems.[10] They had experienced no deep crisis in leaving occupations which had not provided them with many satisfactions; they just sought some leisure pursuits with which to occupy their time.

Inadvertently, they stumbled upon a gold mine. There were many elders in Hidden Valley who welcomed a club for seniors. Baffled by the huge amount of time at their disposition and either unwilling or unable to create meaningful pursuits for themselves, this vast group of old people jumped at the chance to be able to participate in enterprises largely organized by others.[11]

The "seven" found themselves for the first time in their lives in a position that carried both responsibility and prestige. They became the spokesmen and organizers for many of the elderly of Hidden Valley. When the city and the recreation co-ordinator tried to take over the center not only were they en-croaching upon a private territory, but they were stripping the "seven" of the most important role of their lives.

The "seven" fought back at first attempting to do away with the coordinator thus maintaining their position of control, then, when they realized that the coordinator was there to stay, they struck, at times viciously, out of frustration and desperation. Their position slowly lost its responsibility and prestige, but the "seven" kept fighting in an attempt to avoid falling back into obscurity and oblivion. The fight of the "seven" will probably end only with their death, and then the city will have taken over the center completely. It no longer will be a club of elders for the elders, but in a quasi-Orwellian fashion the city will cater to the needs of its senior citizens.

Recalcitrance to Role Loss

The plight of the "seven" is emotionally moving on a human level, while also providing an interesting theoretical case by giving evidence that runs contrary to an important theory on the aged.

Let us briefly review this theory and how it fits to the case just discussed. Irving Rosow studies socialization to old age by relying on the work of Robert K. Merton, specifically upon his role-set theory.[12] According to the role-set theory, there is more than a single role corresponding to a status in our society: A set of associated roles are involved for each status. Rosow applies this general notion to the aged and points out that while there exists a status related to being old, there are no clear roles associated with that status.

Throughout people's lives there exists a continuity of roles and a smoothness of passage from one status to another. A status and the roles associated with it prepare individuals for the next step in life, thus, for instance, being a medical student is a role in a set that is suitable to a position in life while also preparing one for becoming a doctor and ascending to his next position in life.[13]

This continuity of socialization is suddenly disrupted when one reaches old age. Although American people have some anticipations of what to expect in old age, they have no specific training leading to it. As old people they retain the general values and beliefs that they have acquired in life, but no longer have a clear role-set for their new status of being old. The roles of the old are quite ambiguous.[14] Most people find themselves losing some very important roles in society through retirement and widowhood without knowing what to replace them with. This leads to confusion and insecurity in the elders compounded by the negative status generally attributed to old age in our society. Under these conditions, it should cause little surprise that many individuals deny their growing old.

Rosow's work is brilliant in elucidating the distinction between the status and the roles of the elders which lead to the denial of growing old. His work, however, tends to consider roles and their losses too rigidly. For instance, while it is true that some major roles are lost forever in old age, some role losses automatically catapult individuals into another role: A woman's loss of a husband terminates the role of a wife but forces her into that of a widow. Other individuals, such as the "seven," find a new important role, and become extremely recalcitrant when asked to relinquish it.

It must be pointed out that the "seven" do not speak of themselves in terms of role losses and gains but in terms of what they have done and are doing for the center. This is understandable since roles and status are not tangible objects which we carry visibly attached to us but are, instead, rather ambiguous social constructs. To wit:

Most members of this society, however, are not accustomed to analyzing their lives in terms of separate role categories—this concept
is a sociological invention. Therefore, a woman whose husband has
died does not generally recognize the fact that all or most of her
roles are modified. She simply experiences loneliness and frustration
in her relations to others.[15]

Rosow's theory correctly analyzes the plight of many elders
today, and some elders fitting his characterization will be examined later in this work. But not all people go into the sunset
in a confused and quiescent state. The "seven" provide a vivid
example of reaching the meaningful peak of one's life near its
chronological end.[16]

Freed from the burdens of middle-age roles which were tedi-
ously unrewarding, the "seven" are not content to "wait out"
their old age. Although frustrated by their past work experiences, they are still strong products of a "work-ethic" culture.
They seek and find identification in a new activity, directing
the senior club, which allows them to be in the prestigious
position which earlier life had denied them.

It comes as no surprise then, having finally straddled the
horse of success, that the "seven" grasp on and refuse to be
pushed back into the cart of anonymity. They do not meekly
condescend to spend their old age in oblivion but rage violently
in their fight, sparking light on the remainder of their lives.[17]

Growing Old in Different Ways

The remainder of this chapter will focus more specifically
on the individuals who frequent the Corbett Senior Center. It
is no longer the case, as it was for the "seven," that a common
cause overrides individual differences, thus presenting a homogeneous case for analysis. The complexity of the many people
using the center will be harder to capture. No definitive claim
can be made here that the types of seniors described in the
pages that follow are representative of all of the elders at the
center or anywhere else. However, the case histories of the

individuals interviewed show clear, if broad, trends pointing to different ways of growing old.

No typologies were hypothesized prior to going into the field, thus the four types of individuals reported emerge from the data itself.[18] The four types derived, the *relaxers,* the *waiters,* the *joiners,* and the *do-gooders,* were discussed with some of the members of the center, who agreed that these are indeed the kinds of individuals who frequent the center. The data that will follow are only a small representative sample of the many hours spent by the author at the center, losing chess games with sharp-witted old fellows, clumsily learning the steps to the "silver sand" from a nicely attired, frail-looking, white-haired lady, who, once on the dance floor, reminded one of Hitler's bootcamp instructor, or simply listening in quiet amazement to the unravelling of a life story.

The Relaxers

> There was an old person of Bray,
> Who sang through the whole of the day
> To his ducks and his pigs, whom he
>   fed upon figs,
> That valuable person of Bray.[19]

The relaxers show a commonality in their approach to old age. By and large, these individuals have a mellow, peaceful attitude toward growing old; they neither burn with rage nor sit with despair. They choose their schedule of activities and pace of life by engaging in pursuits that have always interested them, or in new projects, or by quietly relaxing, tilling the soil, or watching television. They do not do this to fill the void of empty moments but to enjoy themselves. They tend to be loners or to seek the company of others in informal, loose ways.

The relaxers, not unlike the leisure concept which they characterize, are best described by a series of *nots.* They are not concerned with time, they are not concerned with social pressures to be active, they do not feel the need to work, they do not feel the need to make friends, they do not have the urge to be useful to others.

Significantly, the relaxers are the wealthiest of the people studied (with one exception). These "de Grazia-like" individuals are the closest among the types studied to the modernized classical notion of leisure presented in Chapter 3; they also add new elements to various theories on the aged. These concerns will be discussed after some empirical cases have been shown.

A. Gretchen Kranz. Gretchen was born in 1915 on the island of Rügen in the Baltic Sea. She was, therefore, a Prussian, daughter of a wealthy landowner under a semifeudal system. Gretchen saw little of her parents; she was raised by nursemaids and tutors until the age of twelve. At this time Gretchen passed governmental entrance exams and began attending the University of Rostock, studying political economy and city administration.

A field marshall in the German army, her father grew disenchanted with the Nazi movement and emigrated to Canada with his family. There he worked as an automobile mechanic, thus creating a drastic change of life style for his family.

Gretchen married a Canadian businessman at age nineteen and had three children. When she was thirty-three, the doctors diagnosed that Gretchen had terminal cancer of the colon. By then her marital relationship had drastically deteriorated. Her husband showed no sympathy or support during her illness. Gretchen underwent an operation, survived her cancer, and left her husband. In recounting the events she stated, very matter-of-factly: "I couldn't die, because I had my children to raise."

Gretchen's husband stubbornly refused to grant her a divorce and at various times had her investigated by private detectives. If he could have proved that her behavior was morally reproachable, he would have gained custody of the children. Aware of this threat, Gretchen led a Spartan secluded life. She went to school and learned how to be a court reporter. Later she worked in an office and rose to a managerial position. In the meantime, she had been investing her savings in buying parcels of land.

Time passed and her children grew up to be adults. The two sons moved on to have their own family and their own business (one in the logging industry, the other managing gas stations). When her daughter reached age twenty-three, Gretchen, who was forty-eight, told her that she was old enough to be on her own and sent her on her way.

In 1967 Gretchen decided to move to a warmer climate and sold her land (which brought her $65,000). She worked as a private secretary for one of the owners of Rancho de Oro and became part of his circle of friends. In 1969 the Canadian divorce laws changed, allowing Gretchen to obtain a divorce without her husband's consent. She remarried the same year and lived happily with her new husband, a navy commander.

Gretchen felt tied down by her marriage since it constrained her independence but she found new interest in her life by taking over the redecorating of old houses that her husband bought as a business investment. Gretchen's husband died five years later from the same cancer which had spared her so long ago. Alone once more, Gretchen kept busy for a while managing the transition of the financial matters of her late husband, who in passing away left her $150,000, a new Mercedes Benz, and other holdings. "After taking care of the will and the funeral arrangements, there was nothing to do," said Gretchen.

She soon found new interests in life. She sold her house and moved to a luxurious condominium in Hidden Valley. She takes trips from time to time: Last year she went to Europe, and she spent this past Christmas in Hawaii. She likes to take walks, visit museums, and talk to people. She worked at the center as a volunteer for a few months in order to have a chance to meet and talk to different people. She takes a college class from time to time. She doesn't feel lonely and she is never bored. She stated she does not think about the "deep meaning" of life; she prefers to take it easy, planning day by day. She enjoys being by herself. She doesn't let her friends become too attached because she fears that some of her male friends would attempt to marry her for her money. Asked if she felt that her freedom and attitudes were dependent upon her wealth, Gretchen firmly replied, "If I were poor, I wouldn't stay poor for very long."

Gretchen does not feel old, neither physically nor mentally. Being old to her means giving up on life, living in the past and letting others treat you as a "second-class" person. Gretchen is a small, wiry person, quiet and polite. However, I have seen her tighten her jaws and stand her ground many times when anybody attempted to "get pushy." She feels no social pressure upon her, and she does whatever she likes.

B. Ray Wilson. The next relaxer is a retired lawyer of sixty-five, Mr. Wilson. He lives in a large house in Rancho de Oro, near Hidden Valley, where I went to visit him after meeting him at the center. He doesn't go to the center very often, usually only to borrow or return a few books.

He is tall, slender, white-haired, blue-eyed, and rather athletic looking. He dresses nicely in a casual fashion. He pointed out to me that he used to "dress up" to go to court: "I felt that it would have been a discourtesy to the attorneys, the public, and the court not to be neat." Now, however, he prefers more casual and flamboyant clothing.

Mr. Wilson was raised on his family's ranch in western Texas. His father was an electrical engineer. Mr. Wilson loved to ride the horses on the ranch until his father brought home one of the first manufactured cars which he drove constantly. His love switched again when the family purchased a plane, which he quickly learned how to fly. After World War II he left the ranch and became a lawyer, a profession which he practiced until a couple of years ago.

Mr. Wilson used to be extremely active both in his profession and outside of it. He competed in college track meets and played semiprofessional ice hockey back in the thirties. He still enjoys physical activities but of a different kind. He feels that retirement has given him more time to do the things he likes, and he often goes hunting and fishing. He does not make friends easily, he said, but does not mind since he is basically a loner and loves solitary activities. He thinks nothing of walking fifteen or twenty miles a day while hunting. He also enjoys gardening and reading. He is gathering material for a book which he plans to write "one of these days." Although he is married, he spends a lot of time by himself. He wakes up late in the morning and spends three or four hours by himself in his study drinking coffee and reading, while his wife prefers to read in bed.

Mr. Wilson does not think that he will ever be old as long as he has the intellectual and physical capacities to do what he wants. For Mr. Wilson to be old means to have given up, to have lost the sense of one's importance, regardless of age; one could be old at twenty-five. He is more concerned with physical aging, at times he fears "to become a vegetable like it happened to my mother seven years ago." However, his grandfather and uncles all lived to their late nineties so Mr. Wilson does not worry about it too much.

Growing old is a personal matter for Mr. Wilson: "It is not a matter of age, it's a matter of what you've got up in your head; what your dreams and ambitions are, and a person can either stop and say, now I'm sixty-five, I'm dead, I'm washed up, or you can continue to be interested in what life has to offer and live it to the end."

C. Anne Carter. Mrs. Carter lives on the south side of Rancho de Oro. She owns a beautiful two-bedroom house on a mesa surrounded by some acres of brush-covered land. The house was built by her husband, a building contractor, before he became terminally ill with tuberculosis. Mrs. Carter has been an elementary school teacher for many years in the nearby small town of Verde. "I've been teaching there from so far back," she said, "that I can remember when the schoolhouse was only one room, and we played 'over the top' with the children."

Mrs. Carter is sixty-six, a white-haired lady, dressed in a pretty housedress. She is a small person but does not appear frail at all, has the rugged look of someone who spends a lot of time outdoors, which she does. She has many fruit trees in her garden which she prunes herself; she also cares for the many flower beds which surround the house. On her back porch are two old chairs, which she is in the middle of antiquing.

Mrs. Carter has always been a very active person. She used to be a very popular teacher, many of her old pupils still come to visit her from time to time. She retired in 1962 to care for her husband, who at the time was becoming seriously ill. When he died a year later, she continued living at the house by herself. Although she is alone, she does not feel lonesome or bored. She likes being alone, or rather, with her animals, as she puts it. Her pets are a large cat, and about fifty wild birds, which she feeds every morning. She also keeps a water pond not too far from the house filled with fresh water because: "The coyotes and the other wild animals come to drink at night."

Mrs. Carter was forced to retire because of her husband's health. She thinks of her past with a mixture of sadness for her Jerry, whom she "loved so much" and of pleasure for the days in which she was a teacher. However, she does not live in the past. Mrs. Carter feels that she has adjusted well to her situation and enjoys her house and her activities. She has friends, whom she meets at the Corbett Senior Center every so often. She and her friends usually go out to lunch together and discuss the books that they are reading. She receives many books from a book club; she showed me the book she was reading on Amelia Earheart, which she plans to discuss with her friends at their next meeting.

Mrs. Carter does not feel old, only thinking of her husband reminds her of the passage of time. She feels full of energy and vigor and is happy to be healthy enough to be able to do whatever she likes. She showed me her new golf clubs and told me that last week she had begun taking lessons, because she had always wanted to learn how to play golf but never had the time before.

I had met Mrs. Carter at the center and she was pleased to talk to me. She said she likes to meet people of all different ages and that she is happy when her old students bring their children to visit her. Her ranch is very isolated and it cannot be seen from the road. However, her isolation is not that of a person hiding from life but rather that of a person who has chosen to blend in with the animals and the surrounding country.

D. Dick Porter. Dick was the only person among the relaxers who was not wealthy. He had worked in the credit department in various banks but talking about his past work experiences obviously did not please him. He was very vague about his actual position, but indicated that he had never gone beyond a clerical position. He is sixty-one, and has one more year to wait before receiving social security benefits.

He is a tall, white-haired man, who walks briskly and has a strong, deep voice. He has been retired for only four months. He moved to Hidden Valley from Chicago with his father. His son lives in Hidden Valley, and the three of them lived together for awhile. However, his father did not like the area and returned to Chicago. Dick moved out to be on his own and rented a studio apartment in Hidden Valley. He is quite happy with a small place since he does not want to spend a lot of time maintaining an apartment or a house.

Dick has been a widower for seven years. When I questioned him about how he had reacted to the loss of his wife, Dick said: "Well, aah, you have to adjust, what can I say, you know, I . . . look at it pragmatically and . . . what could I do." He and his wife planned to travel after they retired and Dick plans to go ahead with his plans.

He felt lonely when he retired, but now he likes being alone. At first he missed the security of getting up in the morning and having his day scheduled for him by his work routine and his family life, but he has learned to look forward to awakening in the morning and doing what he likes, creating his daily schedule without having to worry about tomorrow. His comment was: "I was in a rut when I was working, and now I am not. Don't forget that a grave is just a little bit deeper than a rut."

Dick stated that he is a "gregarious person." He likes people although he has no close friends. He likes to go to the city and talk to the tuna fishermen at the wharf or to the park and engage other fellows in conversation. He likes visiting museums but has "no use for clubs." He much prefers to meet and talk with people he encounters on his daily excursions. I met him in the library at the center, where he was borrowing some books;

Dick pointed out that he never went to college but that he likes to read: "You know, I don't read just to do something, I read to learn something."

Dick does not feel old, but he is aware that others consider him old. He pointed to the little things that make one realize that one is growing old, such as when for the first time a young woman stood up to give him her seat on the bus. Dick feels that a person must continue to uphold the thoughts and feelings he has had throughout his life; being old is giving up, talking about aches and pains, being fearful of death. He does not worry about his dying, just hopes not to become a burden on anyone.

E. Otto Bismark. The last relaxer to be presented is a burly, red-faced fellow, with a big grin showing two lower teeth in an empty mouth. He does not go to the center at all. He seldom leaves the house, when he does it is either to go to church with his wife on Sundays or to go to the swap meet. It was through his wife, Edith, that I came to meet Mr. Bismark. Edith is the librarian at the center (see the do-gooders later in this chapter) and at my request she set up a meeting with her husband: "Let me know when you'll be going to visit Otto, I'll have him put on a clean shirt."

Mr. Bismark used to "bust broncos" back in Illinois. He moved west in 1929 when Hidden Valley was but a small village. Once he arrived here, he made a livelihood by engaging in a variety of trades. He worked for a while as a grave digger, then was a deputy sheriff for some time. He used the savings he had brought across country with him to buy chickens, chicken wire and chicken coops, and became a chicken rancher. He did not stop there, but bought some cows and calves, which he began raising and selling.

Mr. Bismark diversified into other enterprises. He tore down and rebuilt old houses, which he then rented. He bought old tractors for $25, repaired them and resold them for $125. One day he gave somebody his old car to be towed away "for nothing," as he puts it. Shortly afterwards, he needed a small part for his car and was charged $35 for it. Seeing a chance to make money, he immediately applied for a license and opened his own wrecking yard, even selling old tires to be recapped on the side.

Now Mr. Bismark is eighty-one. He is one of the richest men in the valley. He owns the land on which Hidden Valley's newest shopping mall, with its Sears, Walker Scott, etc., is built. He owns an entire block downtown where an old shopping center used to be. He owns about 14 miles of land just outside Hidden Valley, plus a score of houses which he rents. His holdings are so vast that a local realtor works full-time administering Mr. Bismark's properties.

In the meantime, Mr. Bismark sits relaxedly in his armchair, wearing an old workshirt stained with dirt (I wonder whether those were his "clean" clothes). He spends his days watching his huge remote-controlled, color television, or rather, as he puts it: "I listen to the Cartwrights and all that until eleven, then I watch the news and go to bed."

He is all alone, since his wife spends the whole day at the center, driving their new Toronado home only to prepare meals for Otto. He no longer drives; the last time his license expired (I suspect some ten years ago) he did not bother renewing it. His beautiful $100,000, red brick house, sits perched on a hill covered with fruit trees. He owns the three acres of land around the house, on which he has a small chicken ranch, plus avocados, oranges, and tangerines. He also has a coop with some doves and a few peacocks running free.

He does not do any of the work on the land, hired hands take care of the chores. Smiling broadly, he told me, "Oh, yes, I walk around the trees, but I don't do nothing." He does not feel old, actually he became upset when I asked him if he felt he was getting old: "I don't feel I'm getting old, every so often someone says, weeelll, Mr. Bismark, are you alive yet? I haven't seen you for a long time, I says, I'm just alive as I ever was." He felt that being old is a state of mind, nothing else. He proudly stated that he has outlived most of his friends, but does not miss them.

Mr. Bismark described his life in terms of prices. He remembered the exact price of things he bought or sold thirty years ago. He enjoys going to the swap meet from time to time with his wife and bargaining over prices. He brings home old things which he restores and displays proudly. He showed me some of his latest conquests, a life-size plastic deer, and an old bell, which he has mounted on a redwood pole in front of the house: "I saw that bell under a pile of junk and I says, how much do you want for that bell? She says, which bell? I moved to cover the bell so she couldn't see it and I says, I'll give you five dollars. . . . Now, I already turned down two $100 offers for that bell." Mr. Bismark apparently hasn't lost that old Midas touch yet.

Theory of Disengagement

The relaxers can now be examined in their relationship to various theories. They provide some evidence bearing on a popular, if often controversial, theory of the aged: the theory of disengagement.

Elaine Cumming and others[20] presented the theory of disengagement, which was an interesting application of the functionalist theory to a particular group: the aged. While previous works on the aged implicitly assumed that society withdraws from people as they grow old, the authors of this theory provided a different hypothesis.

Cumming noticed that older individuals show fewer adaptive capacities and experience a loss of energies. Elders decrease both the intensity and the varieties of interaction in which they engage. Older people progressively reduce their social life space (total range of social interaction measured on a monthly basis).[21] This reduction is accompanied by an increase in absorption with the self rather than absorption with others, since with the diminishing of social contacts, social controls are also reduced. As a result, the elders disengage from deep contacts with others and become satisfied with casual, superficial contacts.

The assumption of previous works that society withdraws from people as they grow old is still standing, what is new is that not only do individuals disengage as they grow old, but that they take an active part in the disengaging process. The theory of disengagement thus states that the process of withdrawal occurs with the mutual cooperation of society and its elders.

The process of disengagement is functional since old people are approaching death and must relinquish their major social roles. Thus, at the time of their demise, society will not suffer from any breakdown, which would occur if a younger individual filling major social roles were to die. To wit: "When a middle-aged, fully-engaged person dies, he leaves many broken ties, and disrupted situations. Disengagement thus freed the old to die without disrupting vital affairs."[22] It thus became a universal functional requisite that persons growing old sever their ties with society. This may occur at different rates of speed and in different degrees, but it nevertheless occurs in every society, claims Cumming.

Cumming accounts for the difference between men and women in the process of growing old. She considers men's roles as instrumental to society (leading to adaptation to the world outside the system) and thus hard to replace in retirement. Women's roles are seen as socio-emotional (leading to inner integration and maintenance of value patterns) and basically the same throughout life, thus allowing for an easier adjustment to old age.

The basic thrust of the theory that disengagement is a mutual process reached through the cooperation of the individual and society is upheld by the data furnished by the relaxers. The individuals studied were not forced to retire. Mr. Bismark slowly tapered off his "instrumental" roles by hiring others to manage his finances and work his orchards. The others willingly relinquished their work roles. Mrs. Carter retired to care for her sick husband, but it was a personal choice since they could easily have afforded to hire a nurse. Furthermore, she made no attempt to return to work in any capacity after her husband's death.

The data also support the point that there is an increase of absorption with the self and that interaction with others becomes more casual. The relaxers prefer being by themselves, or, in Dick's case, only randomly seek others for casual conversation, rather than for forming friendship bonds.

The total decrease in interaction does not stem from a reduction in adaptive capacities but from a deliberate choice. The relaxers are not concerned with maintaining a high level of activity. They are now in a position to choose among a gamut of pursuits and select those which please them.

As for the notion that instrumental roles are harder to replace, the relaxers provide no supportive evidence. Rather, there seems to be some support (Dick being the exception) to claim that fulfilling and remunerative instrumental roles better prepare individuals for retirement.[2][3]

Freedom in the Aged

The slower pace of life of the relaxers in their retired years and the loss of clear-cut roles for individuals whose main enterprise becomes wandering by the pier talking to fishermen, watching Bonanza on television, or feeding hummingbirds, would seem to provide support for the roleless theory of aging presented by Rosow, and examined earlier in this chapter.

However, Rosow considers the fact that there is a lack of socialization into old age as a negative feature of our society. The implicit criticism of society in Rosow's theory is that a functionally regulated society should provide proper training and models for each and every stage of life, including old age. Placing a negative connotation on the rolelessness of old age can be argued on two counts. First, on a purely theoretical basis, one may emphasize, as Cumming does, that disengagement may be functional to society and thus desirable. Second, one may rely on field data and point out that the relaxers do not become roleless due to lack of knowledge of what to do with themselves and their time, but that they enjoy the lack of prescriptions and proscriptions caused by the lack of close societal control and ties.

This is not to say that the relaxers consider their past work role as a constraining burden. Only Dick showed relief from the shackles of an alienating job. The others either found deep satisfaction in their work, as Mr. Wilson and Mrs. Carter, or were able, through their work, to become very successful, as Mr. Bismark and Gretchen.

The lack of correspondence between Rosow's contention that rolelessness is unwanted and negative, and the freedom and happiness of the relaxers can be explained by returning to a previously examined notion of leisure. The relaxers have come as close to the classical notion of leisure as it is possible in our democratic, service-oriented, product-consuming society. In their retired years, the relaxers are able to follow their life-long dreams and escape the iron cage of the work ethic. They have not transcended concerns with material pursuits. Both Max Weber[24] and Sebastian de Grazia[25] in their different ways, would probably agree that someone like Mr. Bismark is very much a prisoner of the work ethic with his preoccupation with money and his orientation toward material goods: indeed, they would see him as a king of materialism, slouched in a throne-like reclining armchair and holding as a scepter a television remote-control gadget.

Nevertheless, old Mr. Bismark and the others have escaped the iron cage of the work ethic since they do not concern themselves with elements which may constrain their freedom: The meaning of their lives is given them by the free pursuit of whatever it is that they want. The relaxers are the paragons of the aged as seen by Talcott Parsons:

> Old age should increasingly come to be defined in consummatory terms. This may be interpreted to mean that, for the individual, it should be the primary period of 'harvest,' when the fruits of his previous instrumental commitments are primarily gathered in. ... This theme is, in a sense, a version of the 'disengagement hypothesis.[26]

Parsons suggests a redefinition of "consummatory" away from the physical prowess and sexual gratification associated with younger individuals toward cultural and intellectual pleasures. Thus, rather than hanging on to middle-age roles or attempt to remain employed in the later stages of life, elders should find satisfaction away from instrumental societal values. Isolation and disengagement when seen in this light are not necessarily negative features but signify withdrawal from the world of work and productivity, in such a fashion as to provide meaning to older years.

Life for the relaxers in unfettered by the ghosts that transform old age into something other than a period of harvest for many elders. Life for the other elders becomes haunted by the four horsemen of the apocalypse, poverty, activity, duty, and social pressure: poverty, since being destitute puts so many dreams out of range; activity, since the compelling need not to be passive thrusts one toward perpetual motion for motion's sake; duty, since the desire to be useful drives one to help whoever is willing to be helped or too weak to reject the helper; and social pressure, since socialized, age-graded ideas of proper behavior deny the joys which one may seek.

The Do-Gooders

> There was an old man of Port Grigor,
> Whose actions were noted for vigour;
> He stood on his head, till his waist-
> coat turned red,
> That eclectic old man of Port Grigor.[27]

The do-gooders see themselves as well-adjusted and happy in their retired years. Thus, it becomes their duty to help other elderly who are not so lucky. The do-gooders are the volunteer workers who serve at the center. They are the Samaritans who give their time and effort to provide services and activities for other elderly. They are librarians, dance teachers, musicians, accountants, etc. While they praise and recommend the services and activities offered by "their" organization, they do not themselves join any club or engage in any of the leisure activities they offer.

They have not, as the relaxers, escaped the work ethic but find meaning for their older years by engaging in an unpaid kind of service which closely resembles work (but is not work since it does not provide for the livelihoods of the individuals; they engage in it freely and willingly, and there is no financial remuneration involved).

The do-gooders feel fulfilled by the endeavor of helping others while simultaneously finding identification and meaning in the roles filled in their helping capacity. Do-gooders identify strongly with other volunteers and even more with the organization at large, while they see other elders as a different group. A "we-they" feeling, is therefore, prevalent among this group.

Theories such as disengagement or consummatory period of one's life are somewhat at a loss with this group, but others are strongly supported by the data gathered on the do-gooders (i.e., Havighurst's activity theory[28] or the work-ethic theory[29]). Before examining the theoretical relevance of the do-gooders, some empirical cases must be examined.

A. Becky Rose. Becky is a venerable old lady with soft white hair, providing a mellow frame for a face mapped by deep lines. As she moves about the center, people greet her, and she replies to all; she seems to know many and has a smile for everyone.

Becky is eighty-six; she was born in 1890. She remembers her past with pleasure although years somehow tend to lose their sharp profile. She has to think hard to remember exact dates, but the feeling and events of the past are lucidly impressed in her mind. She began working when she was sixteen and remembers when she was the first secretary for *Sunset Magazine* in Los Angeles. She still smiles recalling how her boss used to tease her about her clumsiness in operating the adding machine "when they first came out."

She was married for fifty-seven years. Her husband and she bought and managed a hotel in Beverly Hills in 1927. In 1934 they sold the hotel and bought one in Santa Maria, which they sold in 1946. They moved to Hidden Valley, where the husband became a real estate agent and Becky found herself without a job, no longer having a hotel to run. She volunteered her services to some friends who owned a stationery store and helped them for a few years without asking to be paid for her services. She just wanted something to do, as she puts it.

Becky's husband died four years ago, leaving her heartbroken but financially secure. She lives in her own house, which is next door to her unmarried daughter. When she is not at the center, Becky spends her time with her daughter, and they do things together: go shopping, take trips, go to movies, etc. When I asked Becky if and when she felt old, she answered, "I think the only thing that makes you feel old is when you're left alone. You just feel like everything has stopped." She recounted how six years ago her hip broke and she fell.[30] That brought on some feelings of old age, but she quickly dismissed them. However, when her husband died, she suddenly felt very old. Although she lives at home, she has lost all desire to care for her house. She spends three days at the center plus Saturday night when she admits people to the dances. During the days, she usually greets newcomers and tells them about the center.

Becky told me that she loves people and feels that she can help some of the old. Looking around at the center she sees a lot of people who are old: "They are not active at all. Some of them just give up on life, especially men. Women can keep busy sewing and cooking, but there are so many men who do not know what to do with themselves."[31]

Becky stated that she finds meaning in her life by being with people and helping the less fortunate, those who are not financially secure, those who are ill, and those who have given up.

B. Martha Miller. Martha is a volunteer in the library at the center. She told me, with a glint of pride in her eyes, that she is the only one of the volunteers who can type well so she is responsible for the filing cards and the filing system.

Martha worked for twenty-eight years as a secretary for Mobil Oil back in Iowa. When her husband retired in 1952, they travelled around the country trying to decide where to settle. They tried Missouri, then moved to Florida, and finally settled in California.

Martha is a widow now, and has been for ten or fifteen years.

She told me that the company she used to work for was the first to provide an employee retirement plan, so she is now financially secure. Martha doesn't mind at all being retired, "as long as I keep getting my pension every month." She is "fifty-five years old-er" and doesn't feel any different than she did years ago. She has been coming to the center for over a year. She likes serving at the library, "It keeps me busy, I spend all my time here at the center," she said. In fact, she comes to the center three days a week and spends two days at the girls club.

She considers the center a good place to come to: "You know, there are people who are unhappy unless they are with somebody, here, you can meet people if you want to, here." She doesn't feel the need to meet people, she is perfectly happy by herself, but she is happy to help others. No, she said, she doesn't take part in any of the activities, since she is too busy with the filing cards to do anything else.

She "confessed" to me that when she is at home she spends her time watching television: "I'm a television nut, there must be something wrong with me because I keep hearing how terrible the programs are but I think they're pretty good." She doesn't do anything else of importance. She lives in an apartment and she made the point that she doesn't have any flowers or plants; she has no interest in them.

Martha was very proud of the services offered by the center and took some time to describe them in detail. She seemed especially interested in the free dental check-ups so I asked her if she had gone to any, and she replied that she preferred to go to her own dentist, since "here you can't choose your dentist." When I asked her if she spends some of her time reading she said that she didn't, that she just checks the books out to others.

C. Edith Bismark. Edith is the librarian at the center. She is the wife of Otto Bismark, whom we have met before. Edith took classes in library science at a local college, and when the new center was built, she literally begged the coordinator to be allowed to be the librarian. The coordinator was hesitant at first. Although Edith was a wealthy woman, she seemed to have stepped right our of her chicken coops, of which one was reminded by her bodily appearance and aroma. When confronted with the fact that her appearance held her back from the position, Edith changed drastically. She has presented herself in a neat manner since, although she prides herself on buying her clothing at the Goodwill, Salvation Army, or at rummage sales.

Edith is seventy-two. She went to nursing school in Ohio from 1932 to 1935 and became a registered nurse. She worked in various hospitals in Cleveland until 1960 when she married Otto. When she retired, she did not miss her career since her life had a new purpose, that of caring for her husband. Housework, though, soon became boring for her and she began taking classes at a local college.

Edith doesn't have time to engage in any of the activities at the center or to join any club. "My leisure time is at the library," she told me. When at home, she watches the news on television. She also goes to church often. She spends most of her time at the center, going home only to cook meals for Otto. She supervises fifteen volunteers under her and takes charge of the various exhibits the library plans, such as the Bicentennial.

Edith doesn't feel old: "I really don't, I feel so enthusiastic with what I'm doing. . . . Those times when I stopped and thought . . . gee . . . you're really getting old, it was at those times when I didn't have an interest, I was bored." She was beginning to feel old when she was a housewife, but now she loves being at the library; she doesn't consider herself to be working since work is something one has to do, whereas she is at the library because she wants to be there.

Edith feels that the center provides great services to old people. People become old when they no longer have any interest in whatever they are doing, according to Edith, and the center and the library can stimulate new interests.

D. *Tex Wayne.* Tex is an interesting case since he is not yet a do-gooder but wants very much to be one and is directing his efforts to that effect. Tex provides this work with an amazing life story and an excellent example of how the work ethic is still alive and well—in Tex Wayne if nowhere else.

Tex was born in 1918 in Abilene. He has no memories of his parents. He remembers living with an old woman who claimed to be his grandmother, although he finds it hard to believe considering how she treated him. Tex was out in the streets working by the time he was seven. He sold newspapers, washed bottles and caddied at the local golf course on weekends. He had to drop out of school because he was working every day, but he later completed high school while in the army.

Tex's grandmother had a weakness for liquor: "She would take my money away to buy booze, then she would get drunk and beat the hell out of me . . . used to beat me with a window prop . . . I still got knots on my head . . . she was such a mean bitch that when she died, I didn't even go to her funeral."

Often thrown out of the house by his grandmother, Tex ended up by spending a great deal of time at the local whorehouse where the women were nice to him, gave him clothing and a place to sleep. However, the local sheriff charged the madam with contributing to delinquency of a minor and sent Tex back to his grandmother.

He ran away at thirteen and traveled around America by hopping railroad cars. His companions became hobos, who sent Tex out to steal chickens, since being so young he would only risk spending a night in jail if he were caught by the authorities.

On one of these occasions, while spending a night in a Dallas jail for chicken rustling, he met Clyde Barrow. "They had ahhh, Clyde Barrow was in there too, but he, he, at that time he wasn't notorious, he'd done a lot of stuff, but he hadn't started robbing banks . . . that's how I met him. Then I met Bonnie Parker." The twosome offered Tex a job as a get-away driver, and they soon were off robbing banks in Dallas, San Angelo, and San Antonio. The authorities caught Tex in Abilene, and he spent the next few years in a correction camp for juveniles.

Once out of camp Tex, still a minor, lied about his age and joined the army, where he was to stay until 1968. During this period, Tex managed to be decorated a few times, once by General Patton himself. After years of various duties, including fighting in Italy during World War II, he advanced in rank to master sergeant. In 1941 he was married (and still is happily married); he has six children and seven grandchildren.

In 1968 he developed blackout problems due to a head injury and was given a medical discharge by the army. He retired with a good pension. He leased a ranch in California and began raising cattle. He wanted to be away from people, but that soon gave way to a feeling of being isolated and bored. He moved to Hidden Valley and in 1971 began going to college in order to become a para-professional in gerontology and help the elderly. He experienced more blackouts and was confined to a wheelchair for a few years. He did not give up, and as soon as his health improved, returned to college.

Today he has almost achieved his goal of becoming a para-professional. Money is not his object, he says, "I'm doing well financially, but I want to feel useful, to help others." He has no hobbies and belongs to no clubs. He feels useless sitting around, "doin' nothing," and he can't wait to be able to finish his studies and "do somethin' useful."

Activity and the Do-Gooders

The do-gooders are entirely different from the relaxers as they spread much more across different social classes. The wealthy relaxers seemed to express the approach to growing old characteristic of a certain segment of the population while the do-gooders reflect the ingrained values of a culture at large. The do-gooders are the last bastion of a work ethic turned into an activity ethic.[32]

Individuals like Edith only find meaning in their lives when actively doing something, being engaged in a "useful" pursuit. When they are constrained, when they have to bide time by doing housework (Edith) or by going to school (Tex), these individuals are possessed by the notion of the uselessness of leisure, by the negative connotation of unemployment.

In their quest to feel useful the do-gooders replace former work roles with new roles that provide them with activity. The do-gooders provide evidence that not all elders disengage from society and become absorbed with themselves. On the contrary, this group finds its meaning in helping others. The data on the do-gooders provide some support for the activity theory of Robert J. Havighurst.[33]

Havighurst focuses his study on the success of older individuals in their lives rather than on the functional requisites of society as Cumming does. Havighurst directly contrasts his activity theory with the disengagement theory: "Successful aging means the maintenance as far as and as long as possible of the activities and attitudes of middle age."[34]

Havighurst is interested in bettering the destiny of the elderly in our country and offers advice to that effect. His approach to the elders reflects the values of his society: He provides practical, amelioristic counsel while at the same time judging the elders in terms of success.

Success, of course, means activity.[35] Just how activity is defined is not, however, very clear in Havighurst's work. The author himself concedes that "At present a theory of successful aging is an affirmation of certain values."[36]

It is not surprising that Havighurst cannot get beyond very nebulous categories in his attempt to fit his preconceived notions of success to the elderly. Apart from the obvious fault of attempting to graft his own meaning of success onto others, Havighurst falls prey to other assumptions. He equates activity with success, while it has been observed in examining the do-gooders that activity means success only for some, while for others it is just a means to avoid boredom, a way to "keep busy."

Havighurst also confuses activity with engagement.[37] Clearly the two are not the same. Some of the individuals examined thus far in both groups appeared clearly engaged regardless of whether they were active or not, while others like Becky and Martha actively busied themselves without much personal engagement in these activities.[38]

Regardless of the confusion present in the explication of his theory, Havighurst makes the important point that some elders attempt to keep active in their later years. The do-gooders are examples of this, and the next group which will be examined, the joiners, also provides support for the activity theory and ethic, although in a different way.

The Joiners

> There was an old person of Skye,
> Who waltz'd with a Bluebottle fly:
> They buzz'd a sweet tune, to the
>   light of the moon,
> And entranced all the people of Skye.[39]

The joiners are those older people who have decided to spend a large portion of their time and energy to have fun. They feel that they have worked long enough and have no desire to engage in any form of work, paid or volunteer. At first sight, they seem to be the ideal type for the Parsonian notion of "consummatory age." However, they differ remarkably from the relaxers, the group used in this work as an example of old age as a stage of life in which one reaps the benefits of past efforts. The joiners' idea of having fun is directly related to activity in formalized settings: The more clubs one joins, the more travels one embarks upon, the busier one keeps himself, the more fun one seems to have. Activity is thus the key word for this group, activity intended in the strict sense of participating in leisure pursuits organized by others for the benefit of the elderly.

The joiners are tireless in their round of social activities; they appear always clean, smiling, and well-dressed; they are always busy, coming from somewhere and on their way to somewhere. They were, however, quite willing to give their time to me, much more so than any of the other groups. This is understandable since for the joiners social approval is very important, as all of their activities are done with others. Even the way in which a joiner meets other joiners is an organized event, and before examining some individual cases a brief description of this event will be given to set the mood for the joiners and to help understand them.

A. A Get Acquainted Party. A party is organized every other week to allow the many newcomers to become familiar with the various clubs at the center, and to meet other people. The mood of the party is one of camaraderie, of relaxation, and of informality. A large number of people usually participate in these gatherings. The one described here, at which I too was a "newcomer," had seventy-six people. It is easy to know the exact number since a volunteer stands at a folding table near the door leading to the large meeting room, and each newcomer signs his or her name in a log.

Various volunteers and members of various groups are present to organize the event. The newcomers sit in rows of chairs facing a podium where a volunteer cracks a few jokes to set the informal tone and then goes into a description of the center. Then, one by one, we (newcomers) have to stand up and introduce ourselves (people show no apparent surprise when I introduce myself). Standing up gives me a chance to look around, and I see an undulated sea of gray with islands of red and brunette here and there. Most are women, all dressed for the occasion. Next to me sits a beautiful grandmother of eighty-seven, wearing a striking pink pant suit with a matching pink ribbon in her snow-white hair. A few men have come with their wives, just a couple of men are by themselves.

After another speech the volunteer who seems to be in charge of the affair and can speak equally loud with or without a microphone, runs around the room passing a basket of colored eggs. This generates excitement since people are supposed to move around the room and exchange eggs with others while introducing themselves at the same time. One lucky (?) lady ends up with the only large egg and she wins a door prize.

By now the ice is broken, and we all know most of the others, when in come the Swallows in their vivid red jackets. They are seniors from one of the clubs and they play and sing songs for us. I recognize "On Top of Old Smoky" but most of the other songs are unknown to me, while everybody else hums along. The bandleader, who would easily win a Nelson Rockefeller look-alike contest, introduces the oldest member of the band. The eighty-seven year old man comes to the microphone and recites a few poems the morals of which are: make friends, keep active, and look alive.

After the Swallows leave, a lady who could at one time have been a mezzo-soprano sings a few popular German melodies. It is then time for a few more jokes, and a slide show concludes the event. I am the first one to leave the room as people talk to each other and slowly walk toward the exit. Everybody has sat through the whole program, which lasted most of the afternoon. Newcomers know what clubs are available, which ones they might want to join, and most important, they no longer feel like newcomers.

B. Bill Walker. The first time I saw Bill, he was tap-dancing in one of the small rooms of the center and I stopped to admire his rhythm and agility. Thus, I was quite surprised the next day while talking to him, to discover that Bill was seventy-four. He was of medium height, gray-haired and very distinguished looking.

The first time I interviewed him he was wearing a suit and tie. He told me that he was on his way to have passport pictures taken since he and four other people from the travel club were going to Japan on a steamer.

Bill used to work as a designer for General Electric and talks for hours on end about his old job. He worked his way up from draftsman to senior designer. "I could do any damn thing for the company," he proudly states. He worked for forty-two years, and he doesn't miss his job although he has nice memories of it. Bill had worked with bauxite for two years during the war and that affected his lungs. This causes respiratory problems at times so Bill carries around in his wallet a letter from both his doctor and his attorney so that he may be given the proper treatment wherever he may become unconscious. As soon as he retired in 1962, Bill went with a travel club to Mexico, then to Australia. He was on his way to Spain and France when his lungs gave him serious problems, and he had to take it easy for a few years. Bill decided to move to California, and in this warm, dry climate he has felt great ever since.

Bill's love has always been music. When he was working, he spent his free time teaching children how to dance, organizing Saturday shows for his club and taking charge of various parties for his firm. He tried to become a professional dancer, but "his belly got hungry." Bill stated that he made a lot of friends through dancing, was invited to a lot of social functions, and met many young women whom he befriended.

Bill was married three times: "Every time I want flat broke, they were the wrong women for me. . . . Every year I celebrate the day of my last divorce." Bill still likes the company of women, but only socially. He forcefully stated that he will not take any of them to his townhouse. He doesn't spend much time at home, his meals at home consist of frozen TV dinners so he does not have to waste time cooking or washing dishes.

Bill is very happy to be retired since he finally can do all of the things he has always wanted to do. In the mornings Bill practices tap-dancing for about an hour (he places a big board on his rug at home). He then practices his guitar playing for another hour or so. By then it is late enough in the morning to play his marimba without having the neighbors complain. After his practice he is off to the center, where he tap-dances a while longer. The afternoons are devoted to his clubs: Bill plays one instrument for the Song-Melodious group and another for the Sing-Along ensemble. He acts in the plays organized by another group at the center and sometimes he enters tap-dancing contests downtown. He explained to me his routines and the new one he is working on. He invented some new steps in tap-dancing (ankle rolls) and he is very proud of them.

When I posed some questions about growing old, Bill began again telling me about all of the activities he takes part in. He feels very fit and not old at all: "I don't even use any heat at my home, when it gets cold I just tap-dance." He also told me how just last week he played golf against "a bunch of kids," and he won first prize and a trophy.

Bill belongs to many fraternal organizations: He is a Shriner, a Mason, and he belongs to the Commandery. He has made friends at the center and through the orders, but "I've made no special contacts, just kind of fraternal friends. You know, you only go so far." Bill has no relatives left; his best friend is his attorney. He has invested his money in various long-term insurance plans: "You know, when you get annuities, the companies gamble that you're going to die, and I gambled I wasn't and I won." His money, when he dies, will go to the various fraternal orders to sponsor prizes for youth or for organizing yearly banquets.

C. Eva Wood. Eva is an attractive, red-haired lady of sixty-six. She moved to Hidden Valley three years ago when she became a widow. The death of her husband caught her by surprise, and it took her over a year to overcome serious grief and feelings of terrible loneliness. She moved in with her daughter in Hidden Valley but soon realized that her daughter had her own life to lead and bought herself a small house in the country. She also did not like being treated as an old person by her daughter: "You've been around for so long that younger relatives consider you old and you don't feel old."

Eva dropped out of high school as a sophomore and began working in cosmetics, rising to a managerial position. She was married when she was sixteen, and after her husband died she remarried at age forty-two. She retired to raise her son. She is financially comfortable since she has a pension besides her social security.

Eva feels that now is one of the best times of her life. She has no worries: "Well, I could be happier . . . but I'm happy." She struggled hard to overcome the death of her second husband, and coming to the center has helped her: "People here think young, and it helps me think young." She feels sorry for all those lonely widows she sees: "They're looking for a man to go back to the security they had, but there ain't enough men to go around."

Eva has adjusted to being single again. She travels a lot with the travel club, is a member of the club that organizes Saturday-night dances, and spends a lot of her time preparing for the dances. She still finds men very interesting but would not want to remarry. She likes being courted: "It's great to know that you never die."

She becomes very upset when she sees people in their fifties and sixties sitting and doing nothing, being old. Others in their eighties are "peppy," and that really encourages Eva and gives her something to look forward to. Growing old for Eva is in the way people look, think, speak, and above all, the things they do: "The beautiful life is keeping active."

D. Ken Moore. Ken Moore retired six months ago, and moved to Hidden Valley from Omaha, Nebraska. He worked for thirty-eight years as a freight traffic controller for the railroad. He decided to retire at sixty-one because young "college kids" were being promoted while he was not. He is financially comfortable since he receives a good pension from his former employer.

Ken Moore is not yet a joiner but wants to become one soon. He has already joined the pool club and takes part in extramural competition with other teams. The reason he wants to become a joiner is to have something to do. "No," he says, "I am not adjusting well to retirement. I hated my job, but now after working for so long, I have nothing to do; I don't appreciate it at all."

Ken also complains that he does not know anybody since he is new in the area. He lives with his wife and her divorced daughter in a house they are renting. He can't stand having two women around the house and listening to his wife's daughter's problems. He is retired and does not want to be bothered with other people's problems.

I asked Ken if he felt he was becoming old, and he answered, "That question I cannot answer because I retired . . . [pause] like, I am younger now than when I retired." He went on to say that some people when they retire have nothing to look forward to, they just "get sick and die." Ken does not want to end up that way. He told me he wants to join the fishing club and start playing golf; he is also beginning to know some people through the pool club. Some of them are in their eighties and are very active, which gives him something to look forward to. They make him feel young by comparison since he is only in his sixties. Ken concluded the interview by saying, "I'm gonna have to find something to occupy my mind, ahh . . . this is all right but . . . this is just side issues."

E. James Reed. Jim has adjusted to retirement much better than Ken although he has been retired for only a year. Jim is sixty-two and has been divorced for nine years. He is an orphan. Jim became a merchant-marine sailor early in life, then he joined the Navy for a few years. Once out, he worked in a nursery and became so interested in his work that he went to night school and became a landscape designer. He later went into business for himself as a landscape designer and contractor. He is now financially comfortable and has some savings plus his social-security benefits.

Jim is a handsome man, of medium height and with gray hair. He dresses in vivacious, well-matched colors in that expensive but casual look which is so typical of Southern California. He told me that he dressed nicely, not because he is on "an ego trip" but because it expresses a newly found dignity and pride which he now feels.

Jim went on to recount how he had been an alcoholic for a few years after his divorce but that he had found a new female companion, who had helped him pull out "of his drinking habits." She died a year ago and Jim was deeply distraught by it. He just sat for awhile in his apartment. However, he did not return to drinking as the memory of his friend sustained him.

Suddenly he became very lonely in his small apartment: "The nights are very long and lonely, believe me," he told me. So he tried to fill the void left by the departure of his friend and began coming to the center to meet people. He joined a creative writing class, the dance club, and he often goes to the new-comers party to meet new friends.

He feels that he must do more: "I can only fill so much time with writing or coming here, then you go dry or you get restless." Jim does not own a television, he claims that American television caters to people of 14 years of age. He reads a lot and loves meeting people, especially ladies. He smiled and told me that he was in a good position to make "lady friends" since there were not many men to compete with, but he has to watch it since many of them are "after him" to marry him.

His children are all grown up and with families of their own. He visits them every so often. Do his children and other people treat him differently now that he is older? "No, no, actually they look at me with more respect now. They think, he must have done well for himself, he doesn't look too old or broken down yet, they don't think, oh poor daddy." Jim went on to say that if he behaved "old," then people would treat him as old. He doesn't like it when people of fifty or sixty keep talking about their aches and pains and running themselves down with phrases such as, "Oh, I'm such an old bag." People should keep active and do things: "People don't want to know that you're going to pieces and it isn't good for you to relate those things. I think . . . ahh . . . that this overworked phrase . . . to grow old gracefully . . . is . . . is . . . my goal . . . to be careful about it . . . no matter how decrepit . . . [long pause] . . . because it can be a beautiful thing, and . . . and you get deference and respect and you've earned it."

Activity and the Joiners

It has been seen earlier in this chapter that the do-gooders found new meaning in old age by engaging in activities that took the social form of providing a helping hand to other elderly. The joiners have no such amelioristic concept of activity. The newcomer party spells it out clearly; they want to have fun together. And fun they have, from the vertiginous pace of someone like Bill, whose volume and level of activity makes me, chronologically forty years his junior, feel like a decrepit oldster, to somebody like Ken, who is desperately searching new life meaning in activity, to someone like Jim, who is fending away loneliness by keeping busily active.

The others they meet are important but not as individual entities, as friends to be discovered and treasured, only as radiant, smiling faces to surround them in their activities. The joiners are too busy with their activities to stop too long with any one person. This leads to a strange theoretical result. There is strong support for Havighurst's activity theory in this group; success is equated with feeling young, and feeling young depends on being active. But on the other hand, there is also support for the disengagement theory. These individuals are personally disengaged. They have lost ties that bound them to others, either persons or jobs, and are now absorbed in themselves. The others are mere props used to provide the joiners with the meaning or satisfaction they want for themselves.

Thus, ironically, while the primary concern of this group is that of meeting other people and engaging in activities, neither activities nor people matter much. In a frenzy of new activity and in a carousel of new faces, who move too fast to really be recognized, being busy no longer is a means to an end but becomes an end in itself.

Commonsensically, the joiners can be considered a middle-class group. No individual was as wealthy as the relaxers, but on the other hand they were all comfortably self-sufficient financially. They all seemed to have been alienated from society at large either by the death of a loved one, by retirement, or by illness. They all rebounded in the best way they knew: In a society in which activity is success, the best way to make a comeback is through activity. But activity per se was not enough. Having been detached from social ties, they now needed to overcome their feeling of anomie[40] by reintegrating themselves in social groups, thus the clubs at the center proved to be the best vehicle for the joiners.

One of the joiners, James Reed, also provides some information that runs counter to Rosow's roleless theory: Jim feels that he has acquired status in old age as his achievements have gained him the respect of others. Also, the fact that Jim and others choose to retire willingly puts in doubt the claim that all individuals are afraid to face the "second-class" status of old age. Finally, Jim has found a new role in old age, that of "aged Casanova," which became available to him because of his advanced years, and that Jim certainly considers a desirable role.

The Waiters

> There was an old man of Cape Horn
> Who wished he had never been born;
> So he sat on a chair, till he died of
>   despair,
> That dolorous Man of Cape Horn.[4][1]

The last group considered in this chapter, the waiters, is composed of individuals who have given up on life. These individuals have a waiting attitude. They are waiting for death, and some of them cannot understand why they are still alive. The waiting attitude permeates their daily lives and the daily routine becomes a waiting routine; waiting for the center to open, waiting for the coffee to be made, waiting for lunch time, waiting for dinner, etc.

It has been seen in examining the joiners that some people in that group engaged in activities for the purpose of filling in time. Those individuals, however, attempted to maximize the number of activities in a social setting that would allow them to "keep old age at bay." The waiters instead, no longer care for social approval and have given up any pretense to "look young." They dress shabbily and shave rather infrequently. I can say "shave" as I found no women in this group at the center but only men. I checked with the coordinator of the center to confirm my finding in regard to sex and found that indeed waiters at the center are all men. The waiters were also far less numerous than any other group at the center (while the joiners formed the bulk of the members). A few empirical cases will now be examined.[4][2]

A. Tony Paoli. Tony is an old fisherman of Italian descent. He seldom comes to the center. He was here for some legal advice, and I was lucky to stumble upon him. Tony was dressed in an old pair of slacks and a checkered shirt which had been washed many times. He was very reticent in talking to me (as were all of the waiters), but when he discovered that I was from Italy, he changed his attitude and even invited me to his home. Tony lives in a nice house on the fringes of Hidden Valley. He told me that he and his wife moved there five years ago, before he retired, but that with rising taxes he is thinking of moving to a mobile-home court.

Mrs. Paoli is a quiet, retiring housewife. She has always looked after the house and her life-style has not changed with the passage of years. Tony, instead, underwent quite a change when he retired. He had been a tuna fisherman for forty-three years. He started when he was very young, alongside his father, then continued with his own tuna boat.

The sea was his life. He used to be gone for months at a time during the fishing season. He showed me many photo albums of his trips along the South American coast: pictures of rugged sailors, of faraway lands, of different boats. He talked for hours about the sea, the changing boats, the tuna, etc. Tony still looks strong and rugged although he is going to be sixty soon.

He retired because his wife had grown weary of never seeing him and insisted that he retire now that they were comfortable financially. Tony kept fishing for a few years but finally gave in to the pressure from his wife and the worsening of rheumatoid pains caused by years and years of damp ocean air. Tony now bitterly regrets having retired. He has found no new interests. He still wakes up early in the morning as in his seafaring days, but he has nothing to do except wait for his wife to wake up so that they can have breakfast. He takes care of the garden but really has no interest in it; it just gives him something to do.

Tony can not go back go the sea now: "I'm getting too old and my bones have too many aches and pains," he said. He sold his boat when he retired and bought a few apartments which he is now renting, so Tony is confined on land for the rest of his years while his heart is still at sea.

B. George Giddings. George is a permanent fixture of the center. He is to be found in the armchair right outside the pool room and occasionally inside playing a game. George was very reluctant to speak about himself[43] but ready to criticize the center and the people in it.

George is in his mid-sixties. He is a tall, thin, gray-haired fellow. If one could not recognize his physiognomy, one could still identify George by his frayed gray pants and light brown shirt, which he always wears. George used to be a farmer in the Midwest and had his own diversified farm with corn, hogs, etc. He developed arthritis in one hip and could no longer ride the farming machinery, so he retired and moved west to warmer and drier climates. He never married and still lives with his mother.

George likes the center: "It's nice and cool in here," he told me, "I come here twice a day, once in the morning; once in the afternoon." He lives in his house two miles away and drives to the center because of his hip. George is the president of the pool club. This means that he represents the club in the monthly meetings with other club representatives and the co-ordinator. Although the pool club at times has matches with other senior clubs, George doesn't go to the matches away from the Corbett Center.

George doesn't do much of anything else. He occasionally talks with one of the other pool players, but usually just sits in his chair. He told me that he used to play pinochle but that there was controversy with another club over the room and the proper time so he just told them he wasn't going to play any-more. He doesn't take any trips and doesn't belong to any other clubs. He was very upset over the fact that people that weren't seniors could possibly rent one of the rooms in the center. If that actually happened, he said that he would go downtown to the parks and recreation office and complain, "Not that it would do much good," but he would anyway.

C. Phil Matheson. Phil was in his early eighties. He was a smallish, poorly dressed fellow, always wearing a dirty straw hat. His unshaven face often resembled the texture of his hat. His hair was long, greasy, and unkempt. He lived in a trailer court across from the center, but one could be given to doubt-ing whether his trailer had a shower by the looks of Phil.

Phil had been a CPA in his younger years; he owned his own office as well as a large chain of bookkeeping organizations. He had been married a first time for about twenty years. His wife had died and Phil had remarried. He was very much in love with his second wife and had come to depend on her for many things in his life.

Phil's second wife died rather suddenly of cancer ten years ago. He felt that life had dealt him a terrible blow by taking his wife. He became very bitter and felt that everybody had left him and that there was no longer any meaning to his life. He moved to the trailer court and, although he was quite comfortable financially, began coming to the center in a very unkempt way. Phil always sat around with a scowl on his face. He never had a kind word for anybody. He became argumentative and was always right, no matter what the issue.

Phil spoke often of how there was no justice in the world, how nobody ever gave him anything, "I'll be damned if I'm going to give anybody anything," he often said. One day, as I was sitting in the hall, a volunteer came by and approached Phil with the welcome, "Why don't you smile, God loves you." Phil angrily burst into a barrage of curses and lectured the volunteer at length on his skepticism about a God, "There is no God 'cause if there was a God, my wife wouldn't have died." He went on to say that his wife had been a precious being, and a God would not have allowed her to die that way: why bother bathing, putting on clean clothing, why eat, why sleep, why talk to people, why have friends, why do anything, "because this is just a rotten world." Still very angry, Phil said that people are just animals and that he is one of them. He had no present and no future, and was going to die whether we liked it or not.

Phil's relatives had deserted him when he had changed so drastically after his wife's death, and they would have nothing to do with him now. Thus Phil had no one left and no meaning in life. The coordinator, speaking of Phil, told me, "Phil always waited to get into the center, he insisted on his own chair out there (the hall) regardless of how many people there were. He waited until the coffee was made, then sat around until lunch time, when he went home. When he got home, he waited for 'Meals on Wheels' to be delivered to him. He came back and sat in his chair until closing time. At four o'clock he went home and waited until he fell asleep." He would skip the evening meal, eating the hot meal delivered by the volunteers of "Meals on Wheels" and having breakfast at the center, consisting of one-third cup of Cremora, one-third cup of coffee, and one-third cup of hot water.

Last Thanksgiving day, the center provided a large free dinner for the seniors. Phil came over and waited for lunch time. He sat in his chair and fell asleep although the hall was filled with about a hundred seniors waiting for meal time, milling around and talking loudly to each other. A volunteer went over to Phil, took his hand, and asked him if he would stay for Thanksgiving dinner. He replied, "Hell, no!" pulled his straw hat back over his eyes and went back to sleep. By lunch time Phil was gone. The same evening the neighbors called the coordinator informing her that Phil had committed suicide. Phil had gone home, and around six o'clock had telephoned his niece where all of his relatives had gathered for Thanksgiving. He told her over the phone that he had a pistol and was going to kill himself. She dismissed his talk as his usual pessimism then passed the telephone to his brother who, while telling Phil to calm down, heard a shot over the phone. Phil died and left his large estate to his stepdaughter by his second wife, although she had refused to see him after her mother's death.

Waiters and Crisis

There were only a few waiters at the center and their outlook on old age did not stem from being poor, as the findings of Chapter 5 seem to indicate. The waiters at the center shared the fact that they had all worked and been fairly successful in their endeavors. However, they had all undergone crises in their lives, the loss of a work role, a debilitating illness, or the loss of a loved one. The waiters had been unwilling to continue an active life and had disengaged from society.

The waiters strongly support the theory of disengagement which has been presented earlier. Both social contacts and social controls have been greatly reduced in the waiters' lives by their own choice. They neither care about other people nor about their personal appearance or demeanor. They are grumpy, bitter, and sloppy. The fact that the waiters at the center are only men is explainable by Cumming's notion that men lose instrumental roles in society and thus have more difficulties in readjusting to socio-emotional roles, while women have dealt with such roles all of their lives. The case of Tony Paoli certainly exemplifies this theoretical approach.

Rosow's theory also finds some support among the waiters. Crisis seems to catch these individuals unprepared. They are suddenly thrust into a new situation for which they have no guidelines: a widower, a retired person, a sedentary being. Suddenly the old "get up and go" just disappears, leaving but empty shells.

Growing Old and the Life-Cycle Theory

The waiters introduce new data that allow us to address another important theory of aging, the life-cycle theory of Bernice Neugarten.[44] Neugarten rightfully speaks of aging rather than growing old since she wishes to consider the whole life-span, claiming that,

> the effect has been, to speak metaphorically, that as psychologists seated under the same circus tent, some of us who are child psychologists remain seated too close to the entrance and are missing much of the action that is going on in the main ring. Others of us who are gerontologists remain seated too close to the exit. Both groups are missing a view of the whole show.[45]

According to Neugarten, individuals possess certain personality traits and over their life-span they tend, with some adaptations, to retain their personality. Predictions of life satisfaction and levels of activity will, therefore, largely be determined by looking at the aging individuals' personalities. Thus, individuals do not operate according to the structures surrounding them, nor do they follow an intrinsic process of disengagement, rather they behave according to their personality.

Some cases supporting Neugarten's theory readily come to mind. Without returning to the cases in detail, it can be said that individuals such as Gretchen Kranz, Anne Carter, and Ray Wilson are continuing in their retired years a pattern very consonant with their previous personality traits. Gretchen had always been a strong-willed person apt to engage in whatever she pleased. She had been raised as a leader, and her relation with her first husband as well as with her other family members clearly indicated that Gretchen would have been likely to disregard social pressures when growing old and that it was not probable for her to become a waiter. Mrs. Carter and Mr. Wilson also followed inclinations toward pursuits in line with their active, independent characters.

Neugarten's theory finds support in some cases, and her theory is certainly important in its contribution to an understanding of a life-long aging process. However, its attempt to encompass the whole life-span is too formidable an obstacle for a rigorous empirical testing of the theory, at least at present, thus changing the theory into a model of human behavior.[46]

Neugarten presents a developmental theory of aging, which is psychological, not sociological. The theory is very embryonic in its original formulation,[47] but is expanded with articles by Neugarten and others in "The Psychology of the Life Cycle" in *Middle Age and Aging*.[48] In this work are included articles by Erik Erikson[49] and Robert Peck,[50] which describe our life in terms of some rather rigid developmental stages in which our ego undergoes crisis during its identity formation. Doubts about the empirical reliability of the theory are cast by the waiters. Some individuals in this group provide evidence showing how crisis can severely alter the course of one's life. Tony Paoli's retirement and the death of Phil Matheson's second wife changed their individual life-styles from active, successful ones, to lives filled with bitter desperation. This could not have been foreseen by examining the characters before the occurrence of the crisis. The data in Chapter 6 also show how both interaction and setting can be paramount in shaping an individual's life, often regardless of one's previous character.

Graceful Elders

In this chapter four different types of growing old have been discussed. A number of case histories have been presented, and support has been found for various theories of the aged. The disengagement theory was supported in different ways by the relaxers, the waiters, and the joiners. The activity theory was also supported by some data, especially by the do-gooders and the joiners. Parsons' and Neugarten's theories also found some support, however limited. The connection between data and theories was drawn in the body of the chapter and will not be reiterated here.

Two observations should, however, be made at this time. First, by observing the data it is beginning to become clear that the various theories of the aged are not watertight units independent of each other, but that variables such as economic level, crisis in one's life, previous personality, as well as other variables, influence the way in which people grow old. This provides ground for an integration of the theories into a general theory of the aged.

Second, the meaning that leisure has to people shapes the way in which they grow old. The activity ethic has dominated the way in which most of the elders studied view old age. For them, activity is the key to maintaining some sense of worth. However, activity means different things and is seen in different ways and used for different purposes by various individuals. The do-gooders see activity strictly in terms of service for others. On the one hand, the individuals in this group no longer wish to be part of the work force, on the other, they can find no meaning in their lives unless they engage in a service activity. The ingrained notion of the work ethic enables people like Mrs. Edith Bismark and the others to find meaning in their lives only by "belonging" to an organization and providing a "useful" service for society. The joiners view activity as the socially sanctioned varieties of leisure pursuits, which the coordinator and the do-gooders organize for them. They provide minimal input into the structuring and initiating of various pursuits, but once these pursuits are launched, they frantically join them. Activity does not mean for them, as for the relaxers, the reaping of the fruits of the golden age, but provides them with a sword used to fend off the specter of old age. The relaxers too believe that activity is what keeps their lives meaningful. However, activity for this group transcends structured activity in an organized setting. The relaxers take seriously de Grazia's dictum that a holiday is a day to dance in,[51] and their whole life becomes a dance. They dance to their own piper, and are happy whether they engage in socially structured activities, or whether activities are mental ones undertaken in solitary and unsung pursuits. Some relaxers, such as Mr. Bismark and Mr. Porter, have even been able to transcend the notion that activity is needed in order to "stay young." Mr. Porter has accepted the fact that he has grown old and enjoys whatever pleases him personally, regardless of whether it is reading a book or talking to fishermen. Mr. Bismark "listens to the Cartwrights" with no guilt feelings of becoming decrepit. The last group, the waiters, no longer find meaning in either work or leisure. They merely make use of some leisure pursuits, if any, to fill the wasteland that faces them; time becomes an enemy and leisure only a shield.

Chapter 5 will examine a different setting: How poor people grow old in a metropolitan area. The usually dismal picture of the elderly portrayed in the literature will be much more common there. But in leaving the center, I was not filled with a feeling of misery or compassion for most of the old people I had met. The elders were growing old as gracefully as they could; that was their goal, as Mr. Reed had clearly spelled out. Only in the tragedy of Phil Matheson the outer shell of serenity had been punctured and despair had surfaced.

NOTES

1. William Shakespeare, *The Merchant of Venice,* Act I, Scene I.

2. Over 90 percent of my sample was composed of people who had recently moved here from the Midwest and the East Coast. According to the U.S. Bureau of the Census, *Some Demographic Aspects of Aging,* Washington, D.C.: U.S. Government Printing Office, 1973, between 1960 and 1970 425,000 old people moved to California.

3. No precise measurements of income were obtained. The obvious comfort in which people lived, the fact that they owned their house or apartment and other similar and commonsensical factors altogether elevated the seniors of Hidden Valley well over the poverty level.

4. Even the volunteer workers in the center have to be seniors, but since the

facility belongs to the Parks and Recreation Department of Hidden Valley, groups of any age may, in theory, rent a room for their activities. However, in practice, this does not happen. Also, some classes offered are not restricted by age requirements. But a thirty-seven year old woman who joined a pottery class became the object of bitter recrimination by the seniors, who forcefully stated that she had no business being there.

5. The flow of information about the history of the center was pieced together from a variety of interviews with some of the protagonists of the narrative.

6. See "Territoriality: A Neglected Sociological Dimension," in Stanford Lyman and Marvin Scott, *A Sociology of the Absurd.* New York: Appleton-Century-Crofts, 1970.

7. See Georg Simmel, op. cit.

8. Carol Estes, *Community Planning for the Elderly.* Unpublished Ph.D. dissertation, University of California, San Diego, 1972.

9. See Tom Wolfe, *Radical Chick & Mau-Mauing the Flak Catcher.* New York: Bantam, 1971.

10. See the second part of this chapter for individual portraits of this type of elderly and Chapter 5 for an account of poor elders.

11. See the *joiners* later in this chapter.

12. Robert K. Merton, "The Role Set: Problems in Sociological Theory," *British Journal of Sociology* 8 (1957): 106-120.

13. Robert K. Merton, *The Student Physician.* Cambridge, Mass.: Harvard Univ. Press, 1957. For instance, the ambiguity present during the years of medical school is meant to prepare future physicians for the ambiguity of diagnosis.

14. See Irving Rosow, *Socialization to Old Age,* op. cit., for a discussion of studies of behavior appropriate and nonappropriate to the role of the elderly; the studies discover no feature peculiar to old age alone.

15. Helena Znaniecki Lopata, *Widowhood in America,* op. cit., p. 50.

16. See Arnold Rose and W. A. Peterson, *Older People and their Social World.* Philadelphia: F. A. Davis, 1965, for a similar type, which they call "late bloomer."

17. There are other aged, not examined in this work, who are beginning "to rage." Various movements such as "The Gray Panthers" are considering the elderly as a minority group and fighting for their rights, simultaneously finding new life meaning in their cause.

It is my opinion that it will be a long uphill struggle before the elderly become a united subculture (see also Arnold Rose, "The Subculture of the Aging: A Topic for Sociological Research," in B. Neugarten, op. cit.). Just as the blacks came to take pride in their color and culture so the elderly must be able to see themselves as old first and then as men, women, blacks, white, rich, poor, etc. Until wrinkles become a symbol of a group rather than a feared sign of impending doom, a subculture of the aged is but a chimera.

18. See Jerry Jacobs, *Older Persons and Retirement Communities,* op. cit., for a discussion of grounded theory and the elderly.

19. Edward Lear, in Elizabeth Sewell, *The Field of Nonsense.* London: Chatto and Windus, 1952.

20. Cumming, Elaine, Lois R. Dean, David S. Newell, and Isabel McCaffrey, "Disengagement: A Tentative Theory of Aging," *Sociometry* 23 (1960): 23-35; Cumming, Elaine and W. E. Henry, *Growing Old,* op. cit.; Cumming, Elaine, "Further Thoughts on the Theory of Disengagement," op. cit.

21. Elaine Cumming, et al., "Disengagement: A Tentative Theory of Aging," op. cit.

22. Elaine Cumming, "Further Thoughts on the Theory of Disengagement," op. cit., p. 385.

23. Also see E. W. Burgess, L. G. Cordy, P. C. Pineo, and R. T. Thornbury, "Occupational Differences in Attitudes Toward Aging and Retirement," *Journal of Gerontology* 13 (1958): 203-206.

24. Max Weber, op. cit.

25. De Grazia, op. cit., and Chapter 3 of this work.

26. Talcott Parsons, "Old Age as Consummatory Phase," in *The Gerontologist* 3 (1963): 53-54.

27. Edward Lear in Elizabeth Sewell, op. cit.

28. Robert Havighurst, "Successful Aging," op. cit.

29. See Chapter 3 of this work.

30. Among the aged, commonly a bone breaks and then the individual falls rather than vice versa.

31. This quote provides member's support for Elaine Cumming's differentiation between instrumental and socio-emotional roles previously discussed.

32. See Chapter 3 of this work.

33. Robert J. Havighurst, "Successful Aging," op. cit.

34. Ibid., p. 8.

35. See the discussion of activity in Chapter 3.

36. Robert J. Havighurst, op. cit., p. 12.

37. Elaine Cumming notices this confusion in her "Further Thoughts on the Theory of Disengagement," op. cit.

38. See Chapter 3 of this work for a discussion of the various alternatives to leisure and activity.

39. Edward Lear in Elizabeth Sewell, op. cit.

40. Emile Durkheim, op. cit.

41. Edward Lear in Martin Esslin, *The Theater of the Absurd.* Garden City, N.Y.: Anchor, 1969.

42. Chapter 5, dealing with poor elders, examines the *waiters* in detail.

43. After I had spoken to George a few times and thought that I was winning his confidence, the coordinator told me that George had told her to tell that young friend of hers not to come snooping around anymore.

44. Bernice L. Neugarten, *Middle Age and Aging,* op. cit.

45. Ibid., p. 137.

46. For an excellent critique of models versus theories, see Stanford M. Lyman, "The Race Relation Cycle of Robert E. Park," *Pacific Sociological Review* 11 (1968): 16-28.

47. Bernice L. Neugarten, "Personality and Patterns of Aging," op. cit.

48. Bernice L. Neugarten, ed., op. cit.

49. Erik H. Erikson, "Generativity and Ego Integrity," in Neugarten, op. cit. The article deals with Erikson's eight steps of ego development, from infancy to old age.

50. Robert C. Peck, "Psychological Development in the Second Half of Life," in Neugarten, op. cit. Peck subdivides Erickson's eighth state, Ego-Integrity vs. Despair, supposed to cover the last forty years of our life, into various substages of his own.

51. Sebastian de Grazia, op. cit.

Chapter 5

THE POOR ELDERLY

*Shit . . . and you tell me there is justice . . . you go down to the un-
employment office and they tell you you're too old to work . . .
sorry . . . we can't help you . . . who in the hell is gonna help?*

—a respondent

It is the plight of minor characters to go unnoticed. The lime-
lights of life go to the Hamlets while the Rosencrantzes and
Guildensterns move unobserved in the periphery of the stage. In
viewing the tragedy of the melancholic Prince of Denmark one
barely notices the fate of the two minor emissaries. However,
Tom Stoppard in his brilliant play, *Rosencrantz and Guildenstern are Dead,*[1] presents the ventures of the two minor Shake-
spearean characters,[2] while Hamlet is relegated to a minor role.
What emerges in the play is that the lives of the two are made of
the same human stuff, and their fate is just as tragic as that of
their prince.

There are many Rosencrantzes and Guildensterns filling the
walks of everyday life. They are to be found in the halls of
battered buildings listening to the music of bygone days; they
are to be found sitting on grimy benches waiting for buses; they
are to be found in greasy diners eating the $.69 special; they are
to be found in decaying hotel rooms staring at walls; they are
the poor elderly.

In addressing the problems of the elderly, scholars often
speak of poor old people. However, their discussion never goes

beyond providing generalized data, frequently in the form of numerical tables, while the faces of the elderly themselves never come into focus. When they do, it is usually through romanticized accounts presented in the newspaper or in novels.[3]

It is the purpose of this chapter to examine the lives of some poor old people in an attempt to see how the meaning of old age is affected by poorness. This quest entailed spending many research hours sitting on park benches, in hotel lounges, and in recreation halls. My attempts to talk to poor elders were not always successful as a barrier of suspicion and mistrust separate the poor old from other members of society.[4] But when the barrier was passed and the elderly talked, sad tales of loneliness and despair unraveled, making me painfully aware of the plight of some elders. Fortunately, it wasn't always so, and some elders displayed a peaceful and content acceptance of their life station. The various findings will be shown shortly, but before addressing the elderly, a few words about poverty are in order.

The Visibility of Poverty

Once F. Scott Fitzgerald told Hemingway, "The rich are different." Hemingway reportedly replied, "Yes, they have money."[5] What poverty is and who the poor are have been subjects of debate for some time. This debate is hard to resolve since poverty is not a given constant but changes situationally, often depending on the definitions and interests of those who examine it. However, the basic ingredient of poverty can be identified as inequality: "In slightly different words, the basic meaning of poverty is relative deprivation. The poor are deprived in comparison with the comfortable, the affluent, and the opulent."[6]

This deprivation becomes apparent when one notices that the median income of families with 65+ heads was $5,968 in 1972 compared to a median for under 65 headed families of $11,870. The average poverty threshold for an older unrelated individual in 1972 was set at $1,994 while for a couple it was $2,505. Figures for families and unrelated individuals set the percentage for poverty for 1972 respectively at 9.3 and 29.0, while for 65+ families it was 11.6 percent and for unrelated individuals 37.1 percent.[7]

Given the large number of poor elderly one would imagine that it should not be hard to find a number of them willing to talk about their problems. But it isn't so. Oscar Lewis said about the poor that "[they] are marginal people even when they live in the heart of a great city."[8] David Matza holds a similar view and considers the poor as individuals perennially living at the fringes of society and "hard to reach."[9] If the poor are out of the reach of society at large the poor old are prime targets for disengagement[10] from society. This was found to be generally true, as it shall be seen, but disengagement was not always a mutual process between the individual and society.

The Setting

At times, in order to reach some of the disengaged individuals, I made the rounds of old people's homes with a volunteer from a free meal organization and returned to speak to some of the old people, having established an entrée through the volunteer. The favorite place in which I met old people was a senior citizen center which was a far cry from the one described in Chapter 4. This center is located in an old building that seems ready to be torn down any day. A large American flag ornates the dirty brown facade of the building. Some very large picture windows open onto a large room in which six or seven rows of chairs face a dance floor and a worn-out record player.

The rest of the setting is the area between the center and the old square in the heart of skid row. The center is at the fringes of skid row in the old section of town. As one walks from it toward the square, the sights change. In the empty, wind-swept streets around the center there are only a few X-rated theaters, a few cheap bookstores, a religious hangout promising salvation from the evils around, and a few cut-rate clothing stores. As one moves on, the decay of the old part of town gives way to the bright hues of skid row. Along with the colors, the rhythm of the streets changes: They are now filled with people; young sailors seeking forbidden adventures; painted ladies in short skirts and long faces; occasional old men taking a swig from a pint bottle poorly hidden in a brown bag; young fellows eating their lunch straight out of opened cans with oily fingers; and an occasional businessman who strayed two blocks too far from the business district. The buildings are also different. Garish promises of bargains await in the pawnbroker's window; lusty suggestions of sensuality peer through the doors of massage parlors; erotic aids titillate the viewer from the displays of the porno shops; giant electric go-go girls wink on and off at people passing by.

The old square is the heart of skid row. On its far side, across the street, is the business district. Although only a busy intersection away, its life is miles apart from that of the old square. The people in the square are scattered on the green grass by the fountain, sitting on the benches, or just standing around. This is the meeting place for the people in skid row. Shabbily dressed old men with broad, toothless smiles under greasy caps jabber away while eyeing the movement on the square; young black "studs" stand on the corner, "wise" to the whole scene; a few winos recline in stupor on the grass; an emaciated fellow in sneakers, T-shirt and a windbreaker, shifts about nervously; the speaker of the day spreads anathema on the crowd of sinners while the "bums" laugh heartily at his antics, as the show of life on the square goes on.

Waiters

In the midst of this brutally colorful setting many old people try to eke out a living for the remainder of their years. The old are all over the place; they can be seen in every corner and on every bench, but who notices them? They are quiet and unassuming and melt into the background as the Rosencrantzes that they are.

An overwhelming number of the old people downtown are waiters. It has been seen in Chapter 4 that the middle- and upper-class waiters were besieged by personal crises that changed their existence. The waiters downtown also are cursed with a crisis that deeply affects their existence; they are poor. To be sure, for some there are other crisis elements; illness, death of a loved one, etc., but none of them are as preponderant as poorness itself.

Different patterns of waiting emerge among this group of poor, and two basic ones were identified by me. The first pattern is "waiting for Godot"[11] while the second is "waiting for God."[12] The difference between the two and the derived groups is quite simple: The first is composed of people who do not display deep religious beliefs, and who no longer have any strong commitment or meaning in their life activities. The second group of individuals place their faith squarely in an afterlife, thus seeing their present situation as a waiting period to a "better" life.

Waiting for Godot

This group is not a very homogeneous one and the common denominator of their plight is not at first readily apparent since after having lost any deep meaning in life there are innumerable little ways in which these individuals pass the time. Sociologically, these individuals belong to the category of the disengaged, and while some of them claim to have been loners all of their lives, thus lending support to Neugarten's life-cycle theory,[13] most of them have become disengaged without any say in the matter. Some of these individuals at one time have been solid believers in the work ethic while others have always been marginal drifters; in either case, concerns over work and identification with work are remote from their present life situation.

To understand the meaning, or lack of it, that old age holds for this group, sociological notions of aging and of leisure did not prove sufficient. It became necessary to examine the existential relation with which these individuals face life. It must be made clear that while the second group considered speaks overtly of "waiting for God," this first group does not refer to itself as "waiting for Godot." Indeed, many of the members of the group probably have no idea who Godot is and what it stands for. But the essence of their life situation is exactly what Godot symbolizes, the essential act of waiting.[14]

While the human condition of life is one of waiting, regardless of whether one waits for another life or to start a worm farm, as so descriptively put by E. E. Cummings,[15] individuals usually fill their time with various meaningful activities to the point that they become so hurried and busy that they have no time to stop and reflect upon the meaning of their life situation, as suggested by de Grazia.[16]

Far from being hurried, the old people studied in this chapter have become very conscious of the flow of time, thus bringing the need to pass the time to the fore of their lives. Just as the inmates of San Quentin understood the play *Waiting for Godot* quite well when it was performed at their penitentiary,[17] so would the old people considered here; both groups are insiders and experts in coping with the slow unraveling of time.

Thus the main difference between the first pattern of waiting, which has been labeled here "waiting for Godot" and the second pattern, called "waiting for God," is that although both groups are essentially waiting, the individuals following the first pattern have no implicit meaning in their waiting. Cut off from religious roots, far removed from the meaning of work, estranged from their families, and impoverished, these individuals find different ways to pass whatever time they have left on this earth.

Basically, two subgroups have been identified in the "waiting for Godot" pattern. The first busy themselves by magnifying concerns which are usually secondary in one's life: watching television, eating lunch, listening to music. These kinds of activities swell up to fill the empty spaces in the daily lives of these elders and ease the passing of time. The people in the second subgroup fill their time by moving on in journeys with no apparent meaning or goal; they are drifters.

The Sitters

Some individuals from the first subgroup, which shall be called *sitters,* will be examined before presenting some *drifters.*

A. Mary McClure. The first of the individuals in this group is Mrs. McClure. Mrs. McClure lives in a small one-bedroom apartment downtown. Although the tenement is quite old, the apartment is clean and well-kept. Mrs. McClure is a heavy-set lady in her mid-seventies. She sits in an armchair placed two feet away from a new color television set. An old sofa is under the window, in the back one can see a spotless, fairly modern kitchen.

Mrs. McClure speaks as if she were about to cry at any moment. She appears extremely subdued and sighs quite often. She became widowed four years ago. She has a son in the city but he lives far away and his business and his family prevent him from coming to visit often. However, he comes over often enough to manage his mother's financial matters, such as paying light and telephone bills, and the like. Mrs. McClure is not very mobile. She suffers from Parkinson's disease;[18] she has gout and arthritis, and has recently left the hospital where she underwent a mastectomy operation.

When I first walked in, I came with the person in charge of the meal program, who introduced me and left. I had just sat on the sofa under the window when the volunteer bringing the lunch came in. She was an older lady, very nicely dressed, and typical of the do-gooders who were examined in Chapter 4. She addressed Mrs. McClure and asked her about her health with that typical tone of voice which one reserves for good children, obedient dogs, and indigent old people: "And how aaare you today . . . good, isn't it maaaAArvellous!" Fortunately, she left very quickly on her Samaritan route to help others.

Mr. McClure was a carpenter for many years, then both he and his wife worked in a canning factory. When he died, she felt very lonely and still does. I asked her if her husband had left her any savings and she said, "I've used them a long time ago; I'm almost down to my last dollar." She went on to tell me that she lives on $165 a month (Social Security),[19] and that she has to pay her rent, light and telephone bills and meals.[20] She usually manages to make ends meet,[21] but now she has to pay three doctors.[22]

Mrs. McClure told me the story of her life. She used to live with her sister and her six children in the Midwest while her brother-in-law was away. Her sister was stricken and killed by a bolt of lightning, and she raised the six children for four years. When the brother-in-law returned to claim the children, they decided to get married, after which they lived together for forty years until his death. She moved into her present apartment in this city since her sons lives here, but spends her days by herself. She doesn't have any friends in this city and cannot even watch the traffic go by out of her window since it would entail standing up, and she cannot stand for very long. I asked how she spent her days: "Oooh, I have some mending to do, different things . . . but I watch television mostly." A volunteer from a local organization comes once a week to clean her apartment, and she cannot cook because of her shaking hands. I pointed out that her television set was quite nice (it had been turned on all the time, with the volume turned down). Mrs. McClure said that it had been a present just before her husband died. "It keeps me company, maybe I watch it too much, but I have to have some kind of entertainment." She told me, in a broken voice, that she would go out of her mind if she did not have her television since she goes for many days without seeing anybody but the food-service volunteer. As I left, Mrs. McClure was finishing her lunch and turned up the volume on her set.

B. Cecilia Clancy. The next person in this group, Mrs. Clancy, is a regular comer at the senior center downtown. She is a frail-looking woman, who walks hunched over. When I interviewed her, she was wearing an old pink sweater, a checkered skirt, sneakers and bobby socks limp around her ankles. She surprised me by stating that she was sixty-five, since she looks at least ten years older. She speaks with a voice that reminded me of a record player at a faster speed. Mrs. Clancy used to work in clerical positions. She was married and then divorced, has a son in the city, but she rarely sees him. She retired because of heart trouble. Our conversation began in a startling way: (Interviewer) "What did you do after you retired?" (Mrs. Clancy) "Nothing." (Interviewer) "What do you mean, nothing?" (Mrs. Clancy) "I vegetate." She went on to tell me that ten years ago she had a serious heart attack after which she was left unable to walk. She slowly relearned how to walk and now she can walk to the bus stop three blocks away. She is extremely fearful of having another heart attack. "I don't think I could take it. I'd rather die in my sleep than having to face not . . . walking again."

She doesn't miss working, but she is extremely bitter about not having saved any money for her old age. She lives on $270 a month (Social Security) plus a small disability pension, but almost all of her money has to be paid to the boarding house where she is living. She hates the boarding house but that's all she can afford.

> I'd like to get away from there. I don't like to stay there. There are five other people who live there, but they are [pause] their minds have gone, they don't know. This one lady who is ninety years old she, she cries for her mother, she wants her mother to come and take care of her, and [pause] they can't make her believe that her mother isn't alive any more. She is ninety [pause] and, another woman wants to go home to her husband and her children [pause] she wants her daddy and [pause] her mind is gone too.

Bitterly, she told me how she spent too much money on things she did not need when she was well and that she could use that money now to pay for a better place. She bought a violin, at one time; "I love music," she said, and sadly told me she had to sell her violin, and that now she comes to the center to hear music. "I get out of the house; there is just no one to talk to," she continued. She also comes to the center for the bingo game when free prizes are given to the winners; small items are donated by various people, from a can of peaches to a necklace of beads. She doesn't feel lonely, but she misses being able to talk to people, and she comes to the center all the time (I saw her there constantly). I asked her if she considered herself old;

she replied: "I know I'm old." (Interviewer) "Mmmh?" (Mrs. Clancy) "I know I'm old." (Interviewer) "Why?" (Mrs. Clancy) "Well, first of all I look about ninety . . . but I think it's my attitude. I just feel old. I feel like a ninety year old person."

C. Karl Warner. While Mrs. McClure found solace in television programs and Mrs. Clancy listened to music, Mr. Warner has a different approach to filling his days. The paramount concern of his life now is to provide his body with the proper exercise and food. I spoke to him in the vast lobby of an old hotel very close to the old square. The hotel is a huge, three-story building, which caters mostly to old people. Three long lobbies are filled with old men; they are sitting along the walls, not reading, not speaking. The high walls, the chairs, the atmosphere remind one of an old waiting room in a train station. Indeed, these old men are waiting, and most of them do not want to be disturbed by any one while doing so. I sat in a musty armchair next to a wiry gray-haired fellow and attempted to start a conversation. He looked at me briefly, then focused again on the opposite wall, which he obviously found more interesting than my talk about the rainy weather. Wily old researcher that I am, I guessed that he must be hard of hearing, so I yelled out another platitude and smilingly asked, "CAN YOU HEAR ME, OK?" He listened to an explanation of my study for a few minutes in silence then said: "I'm not interested," and returned to studying the wall. I moved down to the next lobby (there are three) and knelt down (since there were no chairs) next to a tall, fairly heavy-set fellow in what could have been a green suit. It turned out to be Mr. Warner, who after reassuring himself that I wasn't selling anything and did not want to borrow money, talked to me for quite a while (until I developed cramps in my legs, to be accurate).

I asked Mr. Warner how old he was and he thought a while: "Oh, about . . . in my seventies." He told me that he hadn't been retired "too awful long," and that "no, he didn't miss working." He worked as a laborer for many years. He had always been a loner; he never married, and always lived by himself. No, he didn't have any friends, but he was acquainted with some of the people in the hotel. When asked what he did with his days, Mr. Warner replied: "I just . . . do quite a bit of walking, get your meals and try to keep cleaned up and try to take care of your health." (Interviewer) "Yeah," (Mr. Warner) "And . . . I think walking is pretty good . . . good exercise." He feels good physically.

> Feel pretty good, no problems with health, can't complain about it too much. Aaah, what gets a lot of these older men that . . . ehh, some of them drink too much and some of them, aahhh, lay around too much, they're stingy about buying enough food; they turn into kind of misers, to keep kind of healthy . . . they go around these . . . some of them even go out to these, aahh . . . church places. . . . They don't buy enough food to build their bodies up.

The question: "What do you do with your days?" was repeated, and Mr. Warner said, "Oh, you've always got somethin' to do, you know, write letters, keep cleaned up. Then you have got to go out to look for certain clothing, keep your health up, keep as neat as you can." (Interviewer) "Do you ever feel lonely?" (Mr. Warner) "No, I don't feel lonely, there is always plenty to do . . . keeping yourself up, keeping yourself going, trying to eat the right food and taking care of your health." (Interviewer) "That gives you enough to do, that's good; what kind of other things do you do?" (Mr. Warner) "Well, I think I just got through explaining it to you." Mr. Warner went on to tell me that he had to carefully go to different cheap restaurants to find different foods to keep healthy.[23] He continued to tell me how these days one cannot trust doctors, but one must look after one's own health. A long dissertation on the demerits of urban renewal followed, and how it destroys cheap restaurants and stores where food to keep oneself healthy can be bought. I then asked if he ever worried about death since he was so concerned about his health. "I never have a thought about it. Never worry about it." (Interviewer) "You don't feel old then?" (Mr. Warner) "NOOO. Of course not!" He went on to elaborate that to be old is not to be healthy or to take care of oneself.

The Sitters Seen Together

The three individuals presented were all very much oriented toward ways in which to carry on day by day. George Orwell once, in recounting his days of poorness, wrote: "You discover boredom and mean complications and the beginning of hunger, but you also discover the great redeeming feature of poverty: the fact that it annihilates the future."[24] When one has to worry about surviving today, one's future orientation tends to become very narrow. In the case of the elders considered here this particular feature of poverty is indeed redeeming: It restrains the old people from thinking about the future for otherwise they would realize that they have no future.

Mrs. McClure and Mrs. Clancy both have a son, who constitutes the last tenuous thread to a family relation. They are both ill and lonely. In both cases, their disengagement is not voluntary, and while Mrs. McClure is practically confined to her apartment, Mrs. Clancy escapes from her hated abode whenever she can. The flickering and sound of a television set fends off loneliness and boredom from the former, while the notes of musical instruments and the chatter of people provide company for the latter. Mr. Warner is not ill and has always been a loner, so for him disengagement is not a problem peculiar to old age. Although he takes daily walks, he is a sitter because he is staying put in his old hotel. New places, urban renewal projects, and any other topics of conversation are only relevant to Mr. Warner insofar as they relate to his health. This old fellow has created a Ptolemaic system of his own in which the center of the universe is his own body and all else revolves around it.

The Drifters

Having had a glimpse into the small world of the sitters it is time to examine those individuals for whom the world does not revolve around the living room and an armchair, but who move on with no other quest but the moving itself, the drifters.

A. Erick Jansen. Mr. Jansen is an ex-ship-builder; he is sixty-six, of medium height, with short-cropped gray hair; he wears slacks, a sport shirt, tennis shoes and a windbreaker, which has seen better days. He came to the United States from Denmark many years ago and has worked up and down the West Coast all the way from Alaska to California.

After being married for twenty years, he has been divorced for a number of years and likes being by himself. He has two daughters in Seattle and every so often he visits them, but not too often as he does not want to interfere with their lives. He knows some of the fellows around here, but he does not have any friends. He claims that he does not want any friends, since he is bothered by the fact that they "watch television all the time" and are always trying to borrow money.

Mr. Jansen lives on social security, and he can manage quite well. He lives at the Gold Coast, the same hotel in which Mr. Warner lives. He pays two dollars a night and does not mind the small room since he does not stay put very long. He knows every cheap hotel up and down the coast and moves along with the seasons. He spends the summers up in Oregon and Washington and comes down to Southern California for the winters. He was upset by the fact that down here hotels will not allow him to keep a hot plate in his room. He is a good fisherman and when up north, he cooks the fish he catches, but not down here, so he does not bother fishing when he is in the south. He eats his meals in small diners and often goes to the Rescue Mission for their free meals. At times he just buys a pint of milk and a sandwich and smuggles them into his hotel room.

He has been retired for four years and has been living in hotels all of the time. Apartments are too expensive, and he would be paying for luxuries he does not really need since he does not plan to stay in one place. Two years ago he bought a Greyhound bus ticket and traveled across America. His comment was: "In every state, it's the same; as soon as you meet a guy he'll ask you for a couple of bucks." He went on to say: "I'm very careful. I don't associate with anybody, except I used to go to dances and meet the ladies." After being asked to say more about this topic, he continued: "I still take out plenty of girls to dances. But I don't get serious." He explained to me that he can't afford to get married again. Wives cost money. A friend of his "made the mistake" of remarrying in his sixties, and now he "is stuck" with his new wife's dental bills. He said that he didn't know any of the "girls" down here, but that he really didn't mind. He was very emphatic about not becoming too close to anybody. He likes to "spend his time" outside and to travel. He said he is lucky to be healthy and feels that people become old because of their attitude of being sorry for themselves. He doesn't worry about things and just takes life as it comes.

B. *Colin Hart.* Mr. Hart is seventy-two. He is very tall, dressed in the usual slacks, shirt, and old windbreaker combination. He told me that he had been a bus driver in New York for forty-one years. He liked his job but, "why work anymore if you can collect a pension?" He "gets along OK" with his pension. He has been retired for seven years. His wife died four years ago and he decided to move around: "For the last three, four years all I've been is riding around different places, different states ... I ... my wife died four years ago and ... I got traveling. ... I just came from Phoenix, Arizona; I was there three, four months, and before that I was in New Mexico, before that I was in Colorado Springs."

He told me that he stays in inexpensive hotels (he is in one downtown right now) and that he keeps moving on because "I get tired after a while of one place." He has a daughter in San Francisco. She is single and would like for him to stay with her, but he doesn't like the city; he may go visit her this summer. After that: "Next winter ... I don't know, I may go to Florida." He discussed for a while the different features of various places, beaches, etc.

I asked him if he enjoys his travels: "I'm not happy, no, I'm not. I was always used to having company. You get tired of this always goin' around by yourself, you know ... sometimes you don't get ... I don't know." He went on to say: "I'm getting tired of it [traveling] now ... you know ... you always see the same thing over a couple of times." He doesn't really know what to do. He is tired of eating bland food in restaurants and wandering about.

While we were talking, the music started again in the center and a very short, gray-haired woman, dressed in a flowery yellow housedress and slippers approached us and asked if either of us wanted to dance. We declined her offer, and I asked Mr. Hart why he did not look for a female companion if he felt lonely. He told me he did not want an old one. "All you see around is . . . (and pointed to some of the old women around laughingly)." He did not feel old until this year when his blood pressure began getting high. He laughed nervously about the fact that whenever he walks for too long, he feels sharp pains in his chest.

C. Frank Rollins. I sat next to an older fellow in his sixties. His sneakers, light pants, and windbreaker showed more grime than usual here at the center. It was early in the morning, and the only people in the center were two or three "old gals" dancing by themselves to a Lawrence Welk record. Mr. Rollins proved to be a very interesting case. He is a drifter, but he is not retired yet. He finds himself in a gray zone; he is too young to retire and collect social security, but too old to find any work. He is sixty-one.

He began telling me that I was wasting my time: "What's the use of studying old people, you're just growing old that's all." After an acrimonious attack on the government and its exploitation of old people and minority groups in general, he answered my question about his work status thus: "Retired? I ain't retired. You retire when you're sixty-two (very exasperated)—I'm a beggar; and a thief. Keepin' my head above water. So I don't believe nothing . . . I've seen it all, I've done everything." He went on some more about the various governmental agencies and how they steal the poor and the elders blind. He pointed to the old volunteer that works in the center as an example. In front of the center the city buses wait for about ten minutes and the drivers often come in for coffee, but they always pay for it. Mr. Rollins complained that they are not senior citizens and have no business being in the center and told me that the volunteer hides the free donuts that are supposed to be for the elderly and gives them to her friends and to the bus drivers (as he was saying so, Mrs. ——— unlocked a cabinet and pulled out a couple of donuts for the bus drivers). Mr. Rollins said, "There is only one way to change the system, start shooting people." He told me that he had been in the military for six years during the war and that now he was not receiving any recognition or financial help from the government.

He zeroed in on the church-run organizations:

The Salvation Army is a big rip-off. All they give you is a bowl of soup. What the hell good is a bowl of soup? You have to listen to somebody get up and whine about Jesus Christ and the Bible and all that bullshit. They want you to get up there and give your soul . . . for what? That bowl of soup doesn't give you enough strength to go from one place to the other for another bowl of soup.

I asked him where he was staying; that he could stay at the Gold Coast for only two dollars a night. He looked at me with a scowl and replied that that was just fine if you had two dollars. He had been spending his nights in bus depots and was trying to find work as a gardener, but that as long as it rained nobody would give him any yard work to do.

He told me that when he would collect social security it probably wouldn't be more than $90 a month because he had never worked at the same job for more than five years.

Never held a job more than five years same place in my life. I've never been fired; I just . . . felt the urge to move on, to search . . . to look for something . . . [long pause]. In the last ten years I had money two or three times, made it and then threw it away. . . . Last two or three years I've been down. I don't know whether it's the situation in this country or whether I'm getting' old, I don't know, I don't understand.

I asked him what he meant by his feeling of getting old.

It sneaks up on you, you're going down the street, and you're a young man feeling good, working at something . . . and all of a sudden, you quit your job and go over to the next town, and there is no job and it hits you between the nose all of a sudden . . . I'm old . . . and then it begins to scare you . . . and . . . it gives deep . . . deep sentiments of things that's coming . . . and then . . . you kind of wish that you'd kept some friends.

He is not afraid of dying, but he does not want to linger in a hospital bed; he'd rather die quickly. He went on to tell me about his feelings of becoming old: "You're going along and somebody will say to you, 'Oh, shut up, old man.' Things are just going fine and then somebody says, 'If you weren't so old I'd pop you in the nose.' " Mr. Rollins sighed and continued: "That's one thing. Another is . . . you used . . . you were attractive to . . . to the opposite sex and all of a sudden . . . they don't even look at you a second time . . . and . . . the . . . you begin to let yourself go . . . it isn't important anymore . . . if this is all there is . . . you know."

Mr. Rollins told me that many of the people he knows just wander from old hotel to old hotel and spend their time looking for bargains like three fried eggs for 69 cents. That is how they grow old.

One day it sneaks up on you. It's like you . . . aaah, it's like a man's sex drive, up to six months ago I had a tremendous sex life, all my life. Then all of a sudden I woke up one time and I don't even really . . . aaah . . . it doesn't bother me anymore. See these gals walking around in mini-skirts that used to give you a feeling of being alive and now I . . . I believe I could see a naked woman and it wouldn't bother me. You lose it . . . see . . . you lose it.

By now it was almost lunch time as we had been talking most of the morning, and many of the elders who had come in while we were talking began to file out to go to a nearby center which serves hot lunches for 50 cents to senior citizens. I asked Mr. Rollins if he was going to eat at the center for 50 cents. He looked at me and said, "They ain't gonna give it to you if you haven't got the 50 cents."

The Drifters Together

The words of the drifters show their position in life only to a certain extent. What really brought the message home were their eyes. The look of frustrated despair given by Mr. Rollins in knowing that it was lunch time, that he was hungry but could not afford to eat, showed his anguish far more than his words. There was nothing romantic about it; it was a far cry from the description of hunger reported in literary account. To wit: "You got very hungry when you did not eat enough in Paris because all the bakery shops had such good things in the windows and people are outside at tables on the sidewalks so that you saw and smelled the food."[2 5] Hemingway's hunger becomes almost an aesthetic pleasure as he procrastinates eating his lunch, which, however, he eats later in the day. Statements like, "I learned to understand Cezanne much better and to truly see how he made landscapes when I was hungry,"[2 6] are sadly out of place when one comes face to face with people who are not delaying their lunch to enjoy it later, but who do not know when their next meal will be.

Robert Park seems right when he states that, "the man whose restless disposition made him a pioneer on the frontier tends to become a 'homeless man'—a hobo and a vagrant—in the modern city,"[2 7] but often there is nothing romantic about the wanderings of modern "pioneers."[2 8] Mr. Jansen shiftily looked around as he spoke, and his travelings are a way to avoid forming permanent attachments to people. Mr. Hart looked very forlorn in telling me about his trips through America, which are but lonesome wanderings from cheap diners to old hotels.

Mr. Jansen is a good example of disengagement as described by Elaine Cumming and her associates[2 9] in that he willingly detaches himself from society and rejects emotional ties. Mr. Rollins, however, although he has been a drifter for all of his life, is now forced to move on by lack of money and jobs, and regrets having no friends. Mr. Hart is somewhat in the middle; he does not like drifting, but does not want to develop close ties, which makes him unhappy about the entire situation.

None of the individuals in this group fits the notion of the work ethic because work provides none of them with a source of identification, none of them miss their work or their work roles. Clearly this group is not composed of either joiners or do-gooders as the group has no concern whatsoever for organized activities. However, one cannot speak of these individuals as relaxers although it may seem that the lack of attachment, and the moving from place to place would put them in this category. The important point that disqualifies them is that they do not travel to enjoy the sights and meet new people, but out of restlessness, discontent, or pure necessity.

Waiting for God

Having discussed those individuals who do not look beyond their daily lives and have little or no concern for the future, it is time to examine some who seem much happier although they are no better off economically than the people examined thus far. These are the individuals who form the group characterized as "Waiting for God."

Most American elders admit to a belief in God and only two to four percent reject religion outright; this trend is typical of most Americans[30] regardless of age. Maves states that

> religion is meaningful to the lives of many older persons as a factor in successful adjustment to aging; but interest in and meaningfulness of religion is not necessarily correlated with age but rather with the continual maintenance of a meaningful relationship between the aging person and a religious group.[31]

This study found Maves' statement to be quite correct; many of the individuals interviewed, who expressed religious feelings, also had ties with religious groups and have been religious for most of their lives. However, while among the middle and upper classes individual religiosity was interspersed with other interests in life, it is among the poor elders that religious devotion is the only meaningful endeavor in life.

A belief in the supernatural frees the poor elderly from the frustrations of their present station in life; they accept their fate with a serene smile in spite of the agony of loneliness and without the fear of failure in some terrestrial role or activity. For these individuals poverty does not destroy the future because the future is beyond poverty; a supreme being will provide for them.[3][2]

Two individual cases will be examined.

A. Sam Park. Sam is a jolly-looking old fellow, the living image of the "little old winemaker." He is short, rather plump, has a huge moustache, a ruddy complexion, and a satisfied smile on his face. He talked in a relaxed fashion and was not in the least suspicious of the researcher. He said that he is seventy-eight and has been retired since he was sixty. He had to retire because his job as a presser in a factory required long hours on his feet, and Sam could no longer stand for very long. He had lost a leg and now has an artificial one, as he told me early in our conversation. He came to the United States from Lithuania when he was twelve and immediately started working hard. He does not regret being retired at all: "I love being retired. It's my golden years. I can't understand some people, they don't like retirement, they wanna work . . . I worked awful hard all my life and now I'm tickled to death this way, I love it."

Sam lives on social security and feels he has no financial problems. He lodges in one of the local downtown hotels; he has a small room and is not too happy about the hotel. Sam told me that there is an awful lot of old tenants that "get drunk all the time" and attributed this to the fact that they are leading the wrong life, a life without Christ. Sam does not feel old and thinks that the others become old because "they feel sorry for themselves. A person should never feel sorry for himself." Sam plays shuffleboard from time to time, but he really enjoys coming to the center and seeing the other people dance. He doesn't dance, not because of his artificial leg, but because of his religious friends. He told me that he belongs to a Christian group with whom he spends his Sundays and that the members of the group are very strict; they do not believe in entertainment such as going to the movies or dancing, so Sam watches the others.

Sam does not have many friends apart from his religious group: "I don't make friends like some people. I don't like it. I like to be by myself." He does not feel lonely. He has been married twice and "buried both wives." He has a married daughter but does not go to see her because he does not like her husband. He also has a son who is a missionary in Mexico and comes back to see Sam a few times during the year.

Sam described a usual daily routine for me. When he rises in the morning, he shaves, reads his Bible for a while, then comes down to the center. He stays in his room as little as possible. "I hate my room, I never stay there." Sam leaves the center at lunch time to go eat his 50 cent lunch at the meal center. After lunch, sometimes he plays shuffleboard, but more often he comes back to the center to watch the dancers. He goes back to his room when the center closes at 4:30 p.m. He listens to a Christian program on his radio then goes down to the hotel lobby for dinner and spends his evening there. He goes back to his room at about 9:30 p.m., turns on the radio to another Christian program, and goes to bed.

Sam feels that a lot of old people "don't understand life. They are tired. They don't understand it. They go to pieces, you know, lots of them." When asked what made him different, Sam replied; "First, because I am a Christian, that's the first thing for a person, to be a Christian." He spent some time telling me about the wonderful radio programs he listens to and his religious group. Finally, I asked Sam if he gave any thought to his future demise. He said, "I don't look to die. I look for the Lord to come."

B. *Nora Simpson*

> *Dear Saviour, keep me sweet today.*
> *Keep me serenely pressing on*
> *Knowing this, dear Savior*
> *Thou hast ordered me to step this way.*

> Nora Simpson
> Written August 1958

> This was given to me by the Lord, a few days before I became paralyzed.

Mrs. Simpson lives in a small studio apartment downtown. I went to visit her with the meal-program volunteer. Her door was not locked, and she lay asleep on the couch. The studio looked pitiful. It was unkempt and smelled of close quarters and dirt. Mrs. Simpson is a small and alert person. She dressed in an old red houserobe and had on a huge plastic and metal green necklace. Her stockings were so shredded that they could have passed as being striped from a distance.

Mrs. Simpson is eighty-one. She has been alone for a long time and feels lonely, but the Lord helps her endure her loneliness. Her husband died twenty years ago, and she has been alone since. Her husband was paralyzed and Mrs. Simpson cared for him for many years. After he died, she turned to volunteer work but was soon to suffer from paralysis herself. She lived with her sister for a while, but the Lord helped her: "That's what the Lord did with my body. I learned to walk. Just like a baby learns to walk." Her husband was self-employed—he trained hunting dogs. He did not contribute to social security so Mrs. Simpson has to rely on Old Age Assistance (she makes $259 a month). She has more than enough to live comfortably on, according to her.

When I asked her how she spends her days, Mrs. Simpson replied, "Oh, I'm so busy. I write all the time. Then I send out my writing." She picked up an old cardboard box from underneath the table and showed me all the religious poems that she has been writing over the years. She told me that she sends them to missionaries and religious groups and that many of them write to her after they receive the poems. Mrs. Simpson gave me a copy of all of her poems, eleven in all, none of them so long that it wouldn't fit on a three by five card.

I asked Mrs. Simpson what else she does besides writing and she told me that she takes small walks to carry the garbage out. She also claimed to have her housework to do and said that she listens to religious programs on the radio. "I used to be an active worker, but since I've been paralyzed . . . I can't be so active . . . but I find plenty to do." I asked her if she was physically well now and she answered, "Oh, I'm all right, but I don't have much equilibrium. But I just trust in the Lord. I believe very strongly in the Lord's healings. I've been healed of paralysis and so many things . . . I trust the Lord." She doesn't have many friends, and she never visits them since she hates to hear gossip and that's all people talk about these days. She goes to church on Sundays and to the bank once a month (she takes a taxi).

Mrs. Simpson doesn't worry about death: "I look forward to the coming of the Lord . . . we don't worry about death because wer're ready to meet the Lord . . . it's so wonderful to be ready to meet the Lord." She has been religious as long as she can remember and spent some time telling me about her past religious experiences and various religious nuances. She was pleased to see the volunteer from the lunch program as a relief from monotony; she sighed, "I might be dying of boredom if I didn't have the Lord to do work for."

The Other Poor

There are other poor old people besides the ones described thus far. These are the ones, who according to Matza, "live in the crevasses" of society.[33] It was not easy to contact the people described here, but others were just out of my reach. Some hotels create an invisible wall between the outside world and their aged tenants. I was quickly asked to leave at a few such places,[34] and the only information available comes through secondary sources or meeting the elders by chance on their rare outings.[35]

One of these hotels is located across the street from the Salvation Army but the old people rarely cross the street to participate in the activities sponsored by this organization. One of the Salvation Army volunteers was telling me that the hotel creates its own little world by providing a cafeteria, indoor mini-golf, shuffleboard, and a color television in the lounge. Two old ladies walked in, and the volunteer took me over to them because they lived in the hotel in question. They had recently started coming to the free movie program after remaining in the hotel, without ever coming out, for a period of five months. The two women did not seem very concerned about their lengthy stay, and when I asked them why they had not come out, they gave reasons such as, "Oh, well, it was too cold to come out," or "Oh, my, time just flies by," or "The streets are so dangerous these days."

Other elderly spend their days in smoke-filled card rooms in skid row. While at first one would think that most of the old people in the card rooms are poor because they are dressed very shabbily, closer investigation revealed different findings. A long conversation with one of the owners of a card room[36] brought to the surface that the card players, mostly old people, have some savings, often quite large, but that they have lost interest in their personal appearance and use their money for gambling.

Other poor elderly drown their sorrow in alcohol. I was able to observe the behavior of some of them and to talk to a few. One of them mumbled to me confidentially, while leaning closer to me that "this little old girl friend of mine can alleviate my blues to a certain extent, but . . . when I get . . . in a depression . . . the only thing that can alleviate is alcohol." Another case was provided by a small, emaciated, raincoat-wearing fellow, who was standing in line waiting for his free meal at one of the local charitable organizations. As he moved in the line, a brown paper bag, obviously containing a bottle of liquor, slipped from his raincoat on to the floor. His "buddy" told him to ignore the bottle because a big, burly fellow who worked for the organization had noticed the bottle and was waiting to see who would pick it up. The little old man bent over anyway and picked the bottle up only to be quickly ejected from the premises. His "buddy," who saw him the next morning at the bloodmobile attempting to sell a pint of blood, asked him why he picked up the bottle and was told that he couldn't resist doing so. Then they both proceeded to give their blood for some money to be exchanged for alcoholic beverages.

These other poor old fit in the pattern of "Waiting for Godot" as they wait out their last years in hotel rooms or attempt to obliterate the ennui of waiting by drinking. These individuals are disengaged and the distance which they have put between themselves and the rest of society allows only a mere glimpse of their lives.

Of Waiters, Poverty, and Old Age

Zarathustra ran across an old man on his way to the city and asked him how he spent his time, to which the old man replied that he sang, laughed, and wept in praise of the Lord. Zarathustra carried on in his journey, marveling at the old man: "Can it be possible! This old saint in the forest has not yet heard that God is dead!"[37] During my journey through that urban forest of skid row I found some old saints who sang the praise of the Lord but also a large number for whom God was dead and for whom all that was left was waiting for their own death.

Mrs. Simpson and Mr. Park as well as other religious individuals, found the strength to cope with the loss of limbs, with paralysis, the death of loved ones, the misery of squalid rooms, and the starkness of poverty. The past had faded away for them; it no longer mattered whether they were hard workers, dedicated to others like Mrs. Simpson, or merely worked to support themselves as did Mr. Park. They were both disengaged at this stage of their lives; Mr. Park by choice and Mrs. Simpson by force, but although they had both become absorbed in their selves, conforming to Elaine Cumming's theory,[38] their absorption was not quite what Cumming had in mind. These people were far from enjoying the ripe fruits of a consummatory age,[39] but rather retreating from the adversity of life to an island where they could wait for God to come and rescue them.

For the others, the sitters and the drifters, such respite was nowhere in sight. Few of them, if any, considered work as the center of their lives. Usually, this group of poor waiters worked to survive and had no regrets about past identification with work roles. But they missed the money they could have saved during their working years or the routine of an organized life.

At this stage of their lives, people like Mr. Hart were forced into the anonymity of rambling on aimlessly. Mr. Hart and Mrs McClure had not been aimless drifters all their lives; they had been pushed into their present situation by circumstances. The others, especially Mr. Rollins, had had life-long cycles of drifting in search of the pot of gold at the end of the rainbow.

Thus, there seems to be no clear-cut theory of aging which can account for all the poor elders. Disengagement seems to be rampant, but it is often forced, rather than chosen. Life factors seem to change the plight of some while others comply nicely with life-cycle theories.[40]

To speak of leisure and leisure time is also very much out of place when one deals with his group. In his work de Grazia differentiates between work time, work-related time, free time, and subsistence time.[41] But among the poor elders, these differences seem meaningless. There no longer is work, and leisure time and subsistence time seem to overlap. Thus, waiting for lunch also becomes the time in which to see other people; deciding what food to eat or what restaurant to go to becomes the main event of a whole day; marginal pursuits which are considered by most of other social members as burdensome or as minor tasks, such as mending clothing, writing letters, or listening to the radio, are stretched to occupy the whole day for this group of people.

The important difference among poor old people, as it was pointed out at the beginning of this chapter, is that for some life has become an existential wasteland to be filled with pursuits to pass the time, while for others life is but an obstacle to overcome on the way to eternal life.

NOTES

1. Tom Stoppard, *Rosencrantz and Guildenstern are Dead.* New York: Grove, 1967.

2. In Tom Stoppard's play the two characters are similar to the point of confusion. Indeed, Hamlet often mistakes one for the other, ironically symbolizing the lack of individuality of minor characters. Recently, an actress suggested to me that

Rosencrantz and Guildenstern are really meant to be two facets of the same person, and that the two parts should be acted by the same person. This would further reduce the individuality of the protagonists.

3. See, for example, Sharon Curtin, *Nobody Ever Died of Old Age,* op. cit.

4. See Appendix.

5. Michael Harrington, *The Other America.* Baltimore: Penguin, 1962.

6. Charles Valentine, *A Culture of Poverty.* Chicago: Univ. of Chicago Press, 1968.

7. *Income and Poverty in 1972–Advance Report* (DHEW Publication No. (OHD) 74-20008.

8. Oscar Lewis, *The Children of Sanchez.* New York: Vintage, 1963: xxvi.

9. David Matza, "The Disreputable Poor," in R. Bendix and S. M. Lipset, eds., *Class, Status, and Power,* op. cit.

10. See Chapter 4 for a discussion of the disengagement theory.

11. Samuel Beckett, op. cit.

12. See the discussion in Chapter 3 of Calvin and his followers.

13. Bernice Neugarten, *Middle Age and Aging,* op. cit.

14. Martin Esslin, op. cit. Interpretations of the meaning of Godot in the literature are by no means clear. Martin Esslin suggests, at one point, that *En Attendant Godot* may allude to Weil's *Attende de Dieu,* thus Godot may in the end be no one else but God. However, what seems clear beyond doubt, and what is meant in this chapter, is that Godot stands for the essential human act of waiting, regardless of what one waits for.

15. E. E. Cummings, "Nobody Loses all the Time," in *100 Selected Poems.* New York: Grove, 1954.

16. Sebastian de Grazia, op. cit.

17. Reported in Martin Esslin, op. cit.

18. The effects of Parkinson's disease are devastating. To wit: "A chronic nervous disease characterized by a fine, slowly spreading tremor, muscular weakness and rigidity and a peculiar gait." *Taber's Cyclopedic Medical Dictionary.* Philadelphia: F. A. Davis Co., 1970.

19. There is a Supplemental Security Income program which brings the minimum monthly income up to $257 (in California). However, many elderly either do not know about the program or are very reluctant to join it since they consider it welfare. For similar findings, see Charles H. Percy, *Growing Old in the Country of the Young,* op. cit., especially p. 20.

20. The meal program charges $2.00 for a hot lunch and a cold snack for dinner (both delivered at lunch time). The meal actually costs the program $2.10 and is prepared by volunteers in local high school kitchens. If the recipients can pay for their meals in full or partially, as most of them insist on doing, fine, else the meals are provided free of charge. Recipients are usually referred by doctors, churches, or other groups.

21. Helena Znaniecki Lopata, op. cit., p. 58, discovered that most widows in Chicago managed to make ends meet by cutting down on their standard of living.

22. Medicare will reassess the doctors bills since it feels that they overcharge and after having reassessed them they pay 80 percent of what they consider a fair charge.

23. The hotel has regulations against eating in rooms. The rooms are slightly larger than a closet, a room costs $50 a month, with a change of linen weekly. Mostly

men are in the hotel, although there are some women who are roomed on the second floor.

24. George Orwell, "From 'Down and Out in Paris and London,' " in *The Orwell Reader*. New York: Harcourt, Brace & World, 1949: 55.

25. Ernest Hemingway, *A Movable Feast*. New York: Scribner's, 1964.

26. Ibid., p. 69.

27. Robert Park in Nels Anderson, *The Hobo*. Chicago: Univ. of Chicago Press, 1923: v.

28. For a romanticized version, see, for example, Woody Guthrie, *Bound for Glory*. New York: Signet, 1943.

29. See Chapter 4.

30. Paul Maves, "Aging, Religion, and the Church," in Clark Tibbits, op. cit.

31. Ibid., p. 743.

32. The serenity of this group reminds one of children waiting for their parents to come home and take care of them. Cf. Freud's statement that, "religion is the childish fantasy that our parents run the universe for our benefit," reported in Peter L. Berger, *A Rumor of Angels*. Garden City, N.Y.: Anchor, 1969: 56.

33. David Matza, "The Disreputable Poor," op. cit.

34. Usually I was told that too many people were attempting to interview the elderly to exploit them and that they were "protecting" them.

35. In discussing one of my rejections as an example to a class in Aging, I discovered that one of my students, a woman in her seventies, had lived in the hotel in question for six months and was able to confirm much of the information I had received by the Salvation Army volunteers.

36. The owner was the husband of one of my students and talked to me only thanks to his wife's insistence. He based his argument that his customers are not poor on his personal knowledge of many of them. He also pointed out that gambling is so expensive that poor old people could not afford it and that the number of customers does not decline toward the end of the month, as it would if they were relying on social-security checks.

37. F. Nietzsche, op. cit.

38. See Chapter 4.

39. Talcott Parsons, "Old Age as a Consummatory Phase," op. cit.

40. See Chapter 4.

41. Sebastian de Grazia, op. cit.

Chapter 6

GROWING OLD BETWEEN WALLS

The patients lined up to get some cake and the band played "Happy Birthday to You" to no one in particular.

—field notes

I had a dream the other day. I dreamed that I was an old man lying on my bed by the window overlooking the front lawn of the building I was in, the Sunny Hill Convalescent Center. Beyond the blue window I could see people in the distance; I could see children running; I could imagine the sound of laughter. I lay there semiawake, listening. I could not quite understand what was going on because you see, like all convalescent-center patients, I was confused. Besides, my roommate was stretched out on his bed hollering with a voice one would never guess could come out of such a thin, emaciated, wrinkled man. He had urinated all over himself again and in the heat of the summer day it was grossly uncomfortable, since any initial cooling sensation which he might have derived from such an action had quickly given way to an intolerable acid stench. He was yelling like a man alone in the middle of an ocean, about to drown, and he well might have as there was no sign of land anywhere to be seen, or in this case, there were no nurses within the horizon.

When I suddenly woke up, I really was at the Sunny Hill Convalescent Center, but fortunately not as a patient. I had taken a summer job at the convalescent center as a janitor (actually, housekeeper was the definition given to my job) with the intention of studying the setting, and coming back later as a researcher, which I did the following summer. This chapter is based on the data gathered in these periods.

Having worked at the center proved very helpful to my research, in three ways. First, I was part of the staff, thus being able to partake in "backstage" interaction.[1] By this I mean that I took part in "gripe sessions"; I listened to the aides' accounts, not in an official form or through formal work relations, but relaxedly over a cup of coffee, from one "low-rank" employee to another. In this fashion I learned how Joe did not have a bowel movement in two days, why Bill was so confused after the new medication, or why that "old bitch" down the hall wouldn't eat unless you pinched her nose closed; things one would not find in records or would not be told to an "outsider." This gave me an understanding of how the aides felt and allowed me to sit right in with them during breaks or to walk around with them while they worked in the center.

Second, I was able to spend time with the patients while cleaning their rooms, and I came to know some of them well. While this does not matter with some patients who would talk to anybody willing to listen, it is important with others, who become suspicious and taciturn.

Third, I viewed the patients as a staff member, thus coming to see the patients in terms of my job. That summer I had a lot of patients classified:

> This one spits on the floor all the time; I'll have to give him a butt can. That one throws his food all over the floor; it'll be hard to mop. Old Anne always had a puddle of urine under her wheelchair. Sarah will walk away with the mop and the bucket if I don't watch her; Dan will talk my leg off so I'll skip his room today.[2]

I came to see the patients as "work objects" rather than as human beings. But I also slowly became aware of other important concerns which made me realize the meaning of growing old between the walls of the convalescent center for the patients. This chapter is not an ethnography of the operations of a convalescent center;[3] it is not a collection of survey data on convalescent centers;[4] it is not a critical indictment of convalescent centers;[5] this chapter intends to explore what happens to the meaning of the "golden years," to the "consummatory period of life" for that handful of elderly[6] who come to "convalesce" in the waning years of their lives. Studying the convalescent center provides support for another major theory of the aged, symbolic interactionism, and it is to this theory that attention shall be turned now in order to provide a conceptual frame for the data that follow.

Symbolic Interactionist Theory

Symbolic Interactionism stems from a major sociological perspective which has found many supporters and innumerable applications. This theory largely originates in the works of George H. Mead,[7] and it is known as symbolic interactionist theory.[8] The application of this theory to the study of the aged is recent, and does not seem to be attributable to one individual alone.[9] However, the first individual to publish an article applying symbolic interactionism to the field of gerontology seems to have been Arnold M. Rose.[10]

The basic points of this theory are the following: (a) An older individual formulates his self-image through interaction with others; (b) his self-image is constantly changed in response to the interaction with others; (c) the most important interactional elements in determining the ways in which a person grows old and experiences his growing old are cultural values and meanings; (d) the way in which a person grows old depends largely on his environment and can be changed by changing the environment. The implications of this theory are important in many ways. The approach emphasizes the importance of environmental conditions on individual behavior, thus providing a theoretical justification for offering professional help to needy aged. It is no accident that symbolic interactionism is the most popular theory among public-agency personnel dealing with the aged.[11] This approach also negates the functionalist assumption of a universal disengagement process and conceives the ways of growing old as characteristic to particular socio-cultural contexts.

Various scholars have emphasized different parts of the theory. Rose's interest is with the ways in which our socio-economic system has placed the elders in a nonparticipatory position,[12] and how changes in our system are modifying the ways in which people grow old. For instance, while retirement now tends to cause disengagement by cutting off individuals from important social roles, the increasing trend toward early retirement may lead to a growing number of people who supposedly become old earlier. However, these people refuse to disengage and reengage in new activities.[13]

Howard S. Becker[14] suggests that changes in adult life should be studied in terms of the situational adjustments that individuals must undergo. Becker does not refer directly to aged individuals, but his suggestion that people react and change in different situations becomes extremely important in studying the aged. It is especially important when examining a situation in which situational adjustments completely encompass daily life, pointed out dramatically by Erving Goffman in *Asylums.*[15] British sociologist Peter Townsend aptly captures the effects of institutionalization in the following quote:

> In the institution people live communally with a minimum or privacy, and yet their relationships with each other are slender. Many subsist in a kind of defensive shell of isolation. Their mobility is restricted, and they have little access to general society. Their social experiences are limited, and the staff leads a rather separate existence from them. They are subtly oriented toward a system in which they submit to orderly routine and lack creative occupation, and cannot exercise much self-determination. They are deprived of intimate family relationships and can rarely find substitutes which are more than a pale imitation of those enjoyed by most people in the general community. The result for the individual seems to be a

gradual process of depersonalization. He may become resigned and depressed and may display no interest in the future or in things not immediately personal. He sometimes becomes apathetic, talks little, and lacks initiative. His personal and toilet habits may deteriorate.[16]

In studying the center the limitations of the setting and the tone and kinds of interactions between the staff and the patients proved time and time again paramount in shaping the destiny of the patients. The interaction observed at times became so eerie that one felt that he was witnessing a twisted play, as if by magic an aged Marquis de Sade had stepped on stage and this were the Clinic de Charenton with its inmates.[17]

The Stage

The proscenium upon which this drama of life is played serves an important function as the setting for the interaction between the staff and the patients. Thus, before being introduced to the actors, as the curtain pulls back, the reader will be presented with a vision of the center itself. The brochure advertising the center reads:

> At the Sunny Hill Convalescent Center the guest wants for nothing . . . screened sunbathing and patio areas, television, telephone facilities, planned recreational activities and beautiful six-acre site are at the disposal of the guests . . . especially noted for the delicious food prepared in the spotless, modern kitchen.

However, as one looks closely around the center, the picture which emerges is quite different. The convalescent center is located in the middle of the small town of Verde, which is about twenty miles away from the nearest city. Although centrally located, the center is isolated from the town because it is situated atop a steep hill, which is accessible only by a road leading to the center; no other building is located on the hill.

The center comprises two wards, situated one below the other on the slope of the hill. The lower ward is a long one-story construction, while the upper one is a two-story building;

both appear fairly new from the outside. The "six-acre" site is indeed there, but the "sunbathing and patio areas" are small and enclosed by a high chain-linked fence.

The inside is almost identical in both wards. It consists of a long corridor running the length of the slightly V-shaped buildings. Rooms with two beds in each are located at both sides of the corridor, with adjoining toilets between two rooms; the same toilet is at times shared by two men in one room and by two women in the next. Both wards have a large recreational lounge, with a view overlooking the town through a large, dark blue-tinted picture window. The recreation lounge is furnished with sofas, armchairs, chairs, and a television set.

Both wards have a kitchen right across from the recreation room. The upstairs kitchen is used only for warming up food, since all the cooking is done in the downstairs kitchen. Small dining rooms are adjacent to the kitchens. The kitchens contain some old, greasy-looking gas stoves, a large sink, a hot water sterilizing unit (for dishes), refrigerators, and other assorted equipment. Both wards have a nursing station, which is a smallish place located behind a long counter. At the end of each corridor is a large bathroom containing a tub and a shower in which the aides wash the patients (four bathrooms in all). The lower ward has a small waiting hall for incoming visitors. This room can be separated from the rest of the ward by a heavily blue-tinted glass sliding door.

The only telephones available are in the offices and nursing station and are to be used only by the staff on official business. I only witnessed a couple of "emergency" personal calls by employees and none whatsoever by patients. All doors are locked at all times, and the staff are forever unlocking and locking doors and closets in their daily rounds. A couple of times the outside door was accidentally left unlocked, and a patient managed to "escape" but was soon found wandering in downtown Verde. One time I saw Wilma, a sixty-year-old ex-ballerina (she had a tracheotomy operation so she cannot speak and has a small hole at the base of her neck), gingerly vault over the high chain fence, and I had to unlock the gate and guide her back inside. One final point: One of my duties was to wash breakfast dishes in the "spotless kitchen," and the only spotless thing about the kitchen were my hands after I had summarily rinsed off a pile of muck-covered plates.

The Actors

Having described the setting, it is time to introduce the cast. The staff consists of an administrator, who manages the facility, a bookkeeper, two janitors, a laundry person, the kitchen staff (a cook, two second-cooks, and part-time helpers), and the nursing staff.

The director of nurses is a registered nurse who is in charge of another nurse and the aides. The other nurse is a licensed vocational nurse managing the lower ward when the registered nurse is in the upper one, which is most of the time. The remainder of the staff is composed of nurse's aides.

The aides are either white women from nearby towns or Indian women from the reservation three miles away. The turnover is great due to the harshness of the job, the extremely low pay, and the nature of the place. I witnessed quite a few cases of aides who left aghast after their first day and never came back. Actually, that almost happened to me, as I was not yet trained in the arts of doing field research while cleaning toilets. There are two kinds of aides: the old "battle axes" who have seen it all, have been there forever, and are not shaken by anything that happens; the others are much younger women, usually fresh out of high school, often on their first job, who live in the town of Verde, where no other jobs are available, or are just filling a gap while waiting for a better job to materialize.

The other people on the payroll as staff members do not work in the center but make periodic visits. There are three doctors, each caring for a certain number of patients, who come by to visit the patients every other week (at the time of the research, the doctors were allowed to bill MediCal twice a month per patient). There are others: a hairdresser, who comes over from the reservation once a week, a social worker, who comes every other week, a handyman, who is on call, and a dietician, who is consulted by telephone.

The rest of the cast is made up of the patients. The patients are not identified in any visible way and are not divided in the wards in any fashion. The only rule is to have two individuals of the same sex in a room, but if one is senile and incontinent and the other is not, it is of no concern to the staff; contingencies such as availability of rooms are much more pressing. Usually the center is filled to capacity, even the room supposed to be used as an emergency room has a patient in it, an old blind wrestler, who must at one time have been a giant, but now has stumps where legs used to be and has lost most of his cognitive ability on various rings across the country years ago.

Not being able to identify the patients at sight[18] was a problem for me, but it was not a problem for the staff, who classified the patients in terms of physical attributes related to their daily work routine. There are the "up and about," those patients who can walk and get in and out of bed by themselves, walk to the dining room for meals, go to the toilet, etc. The others are called "in chair," meaning that they are confined to a wheelchair, and that they must be helped in and out of bed; they need containers to urinate in while sitting in their chair, etc. Another classification is that of "feeders" and "nonfeeders." "Nonfeeders" are those patients (whether "in chair" or "up and about") who are capable of eating in the dining room by themselves, whereas "feeders" need to be hand-fed by an aide. With this system of classification, the nurses and aides can categorize patients in terms of "work time." An "up-and-about nonfeeder" will require little of their time, while an "in-chair feeder" will take a lot more time: He will have to be fed, have his diapers changed, and his bed sores medicated. Most "in-chair" patients spend a lot of time in bed, hence developing bed sores. At one time I wondered out loud why they bothered getting them out of bed at all, and the licensed vocational nurse said that it was required by MediCal that all patients be up and out of bed for at least two hours daily. The classification system is an effective tool in planning one's daily work schedule. This is no different from my classification of patients while I was a janitor (spitter, wet-the-floor type, mess-up-the-toilet type, and so on).

As a researcher, such classification would have proved of little value, since even among "feeders" the difference in people and their behavior was remarkable. It varied from the old woman who was in an advanced state of senility, passively allowed the aide to feed her, and sat staring at some spot in front of her all day long, to the rebellious old woman who would "make faces," close her mouth, throw food on the floor and curse the aide.

The behavior of the patients was markedly different outside of the categories of "work time" invoked by the staff. By this it is meant that categorizing patients in classes based upon the care they require does not account for those periods which place no (or minimal) demands upon the staff. These periods comprise a large part of the day of the patients, and are spent in different ways by them.

Many elderly patients no longer have to worry about the problem of how to occupy their time in meaningful ways because their selves have escaped long ago, leaving behind babbling biological husks which are carted about by unkind hands and spend their time strapped to beds or wheelchairs. But there are others. And it is to these and to their attempts to keep their selves from escaping their weakened frames that attention shall now be paid.

The Interaction

'But I don't want to go among mad people,' Alice remarked. 'Oh, you can't help that,' said the Cat: 'We're all mad here. I'm mad, you're mad.' 'How do you know I'm mad?' said Alice. 'You must be,' said the Cat, 'or you wouldn't have come here.'[19]

The Chesire Cat must have been a convalescent patient at some time or another since its statement to Alice captures the approach to the patients at Sunny Hill. It must be mentioned that Sunny Hill has a mental health license, hence mental patients can be found mixing freely with those whose only fault is to be old.[20] There are three kinds of interaction which are relevant to the understanding that shapes the everyday lives of the patients, staff-to-patient interaction, patient-to-staff interaction, and patient-to-patient interaction.

A. *Staff to Patient.* Staff-to-patient interaction is characterized by what Strauss and Glaser call "work-time."[21] The same problem noticed by the two sociologists in their study of a hospital ward is found at the Sunny Hill center: The patients and the staff's conceptions of time are very often at variance. There are not enough nurse's aides, and they consequently have a very busy work schedule and minimal time to give the patients any attention as human beings; the patients are work objects, as is exemplified by their categorization in terms of work (feeders, etc.).

Given that the staff-to-patient interaction takes place in terms of work, a typical daily work routine will be described. The aides begin getting the patients out of bed and into their wheelchairs at about 6:30 a.m. At 7:00 the day-shift aides come in and finish preparing the patients for breakfast. The aides distribute trays to the patients, who sit in their rooms in their wheelchairs, while the ambulatory cases walk to the dining room. Next, the aides feed the "feeders":

> I was going around with Mary and Glenda feeding the patients. Mary was literally stuffing food in a woman's mouth and the semi-liquid yellowish substance was dribbling down the woman's chin onto her nightgown, which had been washed so many times that it was now an amorphous gray sack.

> Louise was feeding lunch to an old patient and she explained to me that he always refused his water and that was bad for his kidneys. After having finished feeding him she held a glass of water to his mouth which he shut tightly. So Louise turned to me and said, 'See, I told you so' and left making no further effort to give the man a drink.[22]

During breakfast the licensed vocational nurse goes around

with a medicine cart slipping pills in bowls of cornflakes or oatmeal, while the janitor mops up the floor between the chairs, cleaning spilled oatmeal, wheelchair scuffs, and small puddles of urine underneath some of the chairs because the patients requests to go to the toilet are being ignored by the aides. The aides are still feeding "feeders" down the wing somewhere (some patients do not ask for help to go to the toilet anymore, they just urinate in their wheelchairs).

After the chaos of breakfast, with things and people running around, everything calms down. The patients are dressed (or they dress themselves, or are put back in bed) and either sit in their rooms or are wheeled into the lounge room where the television is broadcasting its usual variety of morning quiz shows. The patients look at the television, but most of them are just staring at a box with light and colors:

> I often asked some of the wheelchair patients (the 'better' patients do not come and watch TV) if they liked the program or what program they were watching and either received no reply or something like this—'Bob, is this a good show?' '. . . g . . . o . . . od,' 'What show is this, Bob?' '. . . go . . . o . . . od . . . sh . . . sh . . . ow.'

The 9:00 aide is here now[2][3] and she begins to make beds on her assigned wing. Some days I go around with her:

> Today the 9:00 aide is Louise and I join her. She is making beds in and around patients. As I talk to her she is going right on making beds and talking to me. Some of the patients are up and in the wheelchairs, but others are in bed. Louise picks them up and sits them in a chair, then proceeds to make the beds. After having changed the linen and the plastic sheet, Louise puts the patients back to bed either saying nothing to them or things like—here you go—that's good—, while carrying on a conversation with me or with another aide if there is one nearby.

After the morning activities, the mealtime bedlam of rushing food trays, cleaning up floors, and pushing around patients begins all over. After lunch it is quiet again as some patients are wheeled into the lounge room to watch some soap operas while others are put to bed to take a nap.

At 3:00 p.m. the evening shift comes in while the day shift retires to the dining room to fill in their daily reports on the patients. These reports summarize the activities of the patients in terms of physical and mental functions. Emphasis is given by the aides to things such as b.m.'s (bowel movements) and unusual behavior; since each aide fills only some charts there is a continuous negotiation on whether Billy had a bowel movement today or whether Elma had a quiet day or was restless. The reports are jotted down in about twenty minutes and the charts returned to the nursing station.

These reports are very important for the patients since the nurse in charge compiles her monthly reports by summarizing the aide's reports. The social worker also uses the aides' reports to give her account of the patients, and the various reports are used by the doctors to determine the status of the patients. A doctor comes in, sits behind the nurses' station, and inquires about his breakfast, which is promptly served. Having thumbed through the charts for a while, he walks quickly up and down the corridors, asking from time to time, "How are you today, Mr. Smith, and you Mrs. Jones?" Without waiting for an answer, he keeps on walking. At times he visits one or two patients who may be experiencing serious problems, and then he is gone, not to be seen for another two weeks.

The following is an example of how the information in the reports is acquired in many cases. Mr. Anderson's medical records stated that he had been committed to the convalescent center as a manic-depressive case. The records made mention of the fact that he had been a former patient and had left to go to a boarding house. However, Dr. Bell (his doctor throughout this whole period) brought him back to the center, since Mr. Anderson was in a severe state of depression (listed as spitting and cursing at doctors and nurses).

I thumbed through the reports of the aides and found that Mr. Anderson was often reported as "depressed" (aides have five choices in their chart: satisfactory, confused, depressed, irritable, noisy). On the back of the report, under "nurses' progress notes" it was often generally stated that Mr. Anderson had shown signs of depression, and occasionally he was reported as having said things such as, "If I had a gun I would shoot myself."

I happened to be present during one of Mr. Anderson's "depressive" conditions.

> Mr. Anderson said that he could not understand why they locked the windows, that all it would take to get out would be a kitchen knife used as a screwdriver. The aide wrote down in her report that he was very agitated and talked about escaping from the center.

My impression of the "incident" was entirely different. I had heard Mr. Anderson make the comment about the windows to an aide.[24] The incident assumed new meaning in the aide's account of it. Dramatic overtones kept piling on until what had seemed to me a frustrated remark about the futility of certain security measures became a dramatic plan to escape from the center. The incident shows that the interpretation of Mr. Anderson's behavior as deviant was taken by an aide who had a preconceived notion of his depression and was in a hurry to finish her report. Her account became of extreme importance since the other members of the staff rely solely upon such reports to pass judgment on the patients.

After this example of "form filling," it is time to return to the daily scheduled events. The daily work routine is now in the hands of the evening shift. The circle starts all over again—getting patients up from their naps, making beds, getting patients ready for dinner. It is 5:00 p.m., the last meal of the day, the last moment of a kaleidoscope of colors, odors, noises: Food is served, forced into mouths, spat out, cleaned up, dropped on the floor, aides yell at patients, and patients scream in the hall, in their rooms, in their chairs, and then, silence again. Some patients, a few, walk back to the lounge room, the others are put to bed, the day at the center is over.

The rush imposed by a heavy work load leads the aides to treat the patients in the same fashion: It becomes legitimate to stuff food down their throats because the goal has become serving the meal, not nourishing the patient, or to lift them in and out of bed as if they were inanimate dummies because the goal is bed making not making the patient comfortable. The patients thus end up suffering from "organization contingencies" similar to those found by many sociologists in other settings.[2][5] But what is suffering here from problems stemming from work-flow contingencies is not a car malfunctioning from shoddy workmanship, but human beings who by being treated as inanimate objects end up becoming inanimate objects.

B. Patient to Staff. Patients find themselves competing for the staff's attention. The patients are not rushed by a busy work schedule, on the contrary they have nothing but time on their hands. Apart from the scheduled rounds of activities such as meals, baths, haircuts, etc. there are scarcely any other goings-on available to the patients. The patients who still have the physical and mental capabilities to do so return to their rooms after the scheduled activities are over; others never leave their room; the rest, who fall somewhere in between, are carted to the recreation room to watch television.

Confined to a restricted setting, beyond their control, the patients attempt to break the monotony of the empty periods of waiting for the next scheduled activity. The patients employ various strategies to attract the attention of the aides. They wave their hands or call the aides by their first names; one of the patients kept calling to me "curly," but after a while I realized he was saying "girly" since he was almost blind and assumed that the person walking by was an aide. "Bob waves his hand at the aide who is passing by and mumbles—toilet—she looks at him and says—oh you don't have to go—and goes on." When they attract someone's attention, usually a new aide or me, they smile and ask for a glass of water (or milk) or for a dime to buy a Coke. Five minutes later, up goes the same hand, and the same person asks for another glass of water. Doing beds or cleaning rooms is also a good time to attempt to engage the aide in conversation because she cannot just turn around and leave. These attempts to create diversions in the period between meals, or between a meal and a bath, are treated by the staff unanimously in the same fashion—they are ignored unless they become a problem which will disrupt the daily schedule; things such as a patient defecating in the hallway or pulling another patient's hair can no longer be ignored as they would soon attract the attention of the licensed vocational nurse or the administrator.

C. Patient to Patient. In examining the two previous kinds of interaction it was found that interaction between staff and patients was characterized by a work schedule and that between patients and staff by attention on one side and disinterest on the other side. The interaction among patients is mainly characterized by its absence. Patients do not have anything to do with each other. To fraternize with other patients would mean to place oneself at their level, to admit that one indeed belongs here.

Thus, the others are ignored. Once I asked Al, who was a great sports fan, why he did not watch the ball games on television. He replied that he would not go into the recreation room during the day because he did not like to see and smell the result of other incontinent patients, and the aides would not let him watch the night games.

I was talking to Mr. Anderson, who was so talkative that I wondered why he did not speak to his fellow patients. He said that there was nobody to talk to because they were all senile or crazy. This was said right in front of Mr. Stern, his roommate, who had turned his wheelchair away from us and seemed very absorbed in a magazine, but who was really listening to our conversation since he was not turning the pages of his magazine.

At Christmas I had sent Mr. Adams a set of checkers, and when I returned to the center the next summer, he invited me to play with him. The checker set had not been opened yet, and Mr. Adams said that there was nobody to play with at the center. Later I discovered that this was not true since I played with other patients. When I mentioned this to Mr. Adams, he claimed that they were not good enough players to play with him. But neither was I, because after an initial doubt as to whether I should let "poor old Mr. Adams" beat me at checkers, I realized that I had as much of a chance of beating him at checkers as I would have had of spotting Bobby Fischer a rook and then beating him at chess.

When interaction between patients does take place, it is not of a desirable kind. The following examples illustrate this point. The administrator decided to put Mr. Adams and Mr. Ritter, two of the "better" patients, in the same room. This arrangement did not last long. Both fellows liked their privacy and the freedom of doing what they liked in their rooms. They were known to become easily irritated by other patients and to keep to themselves most of the time. They tolerated each other for a while but began complaining about each other's quirks privately (often to me). The complaints were mostly about things such as, "It's hard to understand him, he stutters," or "He's always listening to that damn radio and it bothers me." This eventually led to open confrontation, which occurred when they were both listening to their favorite program on their transistor radios and tried to outdo each other by a battle of volumes. The nurse rushed in to see what was going on, and as a result Mr. Adams went back upstairs to a new room.

This was where I left him. He was rooming with a wheelchair/incontinent patient (almost paralyzed by a stroke and unable to speak). Mr. Adams preferred it that way since he was practically by himself in the room. He had more personal possessions than most patients; he had a radio, an alarm clock/barometer, which he had put together himself (as he often told me), and the most prized of all—an armchair which reclined in three positions.

At times, the interaction between patients became violent as when somebody grabbed hold of a hank of hair and pulled as hard as he or she could. A couple of times punches were thrown by some patients, but these flare-ups were rare. What caused most of the problems was the mixing of mental cases with normal patients as shown by the following example.

Mr. Reid, an obtrusive, large fellow in his late fifties, had been declared insane by the courts following a bout with the law over a charge of attempted rape. He had been on his best behavior, and his improvement had gained him a transfer from the county mental institution to the Sunny Hill Convalescent Center.

Mr. Reid did not show signs of improving when he reached the center, on the contrary, he managed to alienate the young aides by continually exposing his genitalia and propositioning them. The old "battle axes" just laughed at his antics, and they laughed even harder when we found him in a bathroom while Wilma, the ex-ballerina patient, was performing fellatio on him. It was assumed that she had been a willing partner, and jokes about it stirred laughter and crassness.

Two months later, the laughter turned hollow with tragedy when the night aide discoverdd Mr. Rooney, the quiet, thin elder who roomed with Mr. Reid, dying in agony while "every orifice in his body was bleeding," as the nurse puts it. Then and only then, was Mr. Reid sent back to the county medical institution.

The Prisoners

"There is a good deal to be said for internment. It keeps you out of the saloon and helps you to keep up with your reading."[26] P. G. Wodehouse took his confinement to a lunatic asylum by the Nazis with a humor worthy of his novels. Some of the patients at the center would certainly agree that internment keeps you out of the saloons, as a matter of fact, that was exactly why some of them were there. They would also agree that there is plenty of time to keep up with one's reading, but they would not sound as pleased about it as Wodehouse did.

The patients respond in different ways to their confinement in the center. Those who manage to survive the heavy odds against them and retain a lucid mind are few indeed. They may or may not have reconciled themselves with spending the remainder of their days at the center, but they all agree that their stay is against their will, that they are for all practical purposes being kept prisoners in the center.

Mr. Anderson is a tall, thin man in his early eighties; his vivid, alert eyes peer at you from above his hollow cheeks, and his long, bony hands are tightly held in his lap. He walks slowly, slightly hunched, but he walks.

Mr. Anderson used to live in a boarding house. One day the people who managed the house told him that he had to go to the doctor for a check-up. He was taken to the center and has been there ever since. He feels that this is illegal, and that the doctor signed his release to the center because he is a good patient, ambulatory and quiet, and they wanted his money. He has written to his daughter about it but has received no reply.

Mr. Anderson told me his story in a calm, resigned manner. He feels as if he were in a prison. He spends his days voraciously reading old novels and magazines. Mr. Anderson said that when he reads he loses track of time and before he knows it, it is time for lunch or dinner. At times, however, he feels very depressed about being in the convalescent center, then he closes the door and stares out of the window since he doesn't feel like reading.

Mr. Ritter, a tall, heavy-set fellow in his late fifties, is another case. He used to be a minor-league pitcher and he went on to become a professional heavy-weight fighter. He has pictures of himself and his brother (a fighter also) in their boxing attire. Mr. Ritter told me about his fights, the most famous one being against Jim Braddock. His left ear, with its "cauliflower" look, testifies to his fighting years. He likes to talk about his boxing days—the ring, the victories, the ones that got away, and the traveling from city to city between fights.

Mr. Ritter's chart tells its readers that he has a psychotic mental disorder caused by chronic alcoholism. He was placed in custody in 1971 as decreed by court order after psychiatric examination. The examiner reported, as can be read in the chart, that Mr. Ritter was confused. He had trouble subtracting numbers from 100 in descending order, seven at a time (he became confused at 93). He also forgot to mention Kennedy when listing our presidents backward. The examiner's report in 1972 showed no signs of progress; instead, Mr. Ritter had become more confused, at least according to the test. He has to be reexamined every year to determine whether his mental state warrants commitment. While no cure or therapy is prescribed for Mr. Ritter, he is being administered quite a few phenobarbital drugs as sedatives on an "as-needed" basis.

Mr. Ritter blames his sister-in-law for having been committed, unjustly in his opinion. He says that he was in his trailer when a couple of sheriff deputies came over and asked him to go for a ride with them. The next thing he knew, he was in the courthouse, and these fellows in white coats kept asking him funny questions and writing down something on a pad before he had a chance to answer. From there, he was taken to a boarding house where he stayed for a year, without liking it very much, and finally he was transferred to the convalescent center without being given any explanation for the move. Mr. Ritter feels that he is being kept at the center as a captive, but he is resigned and he will not attempt to escape. He spends his days mending old trousers or sewing buttons on shirts and listens to the radio from time to time.

The last case examined is Mr. Adams who is not resigned to spending the rest of his life at the center. He kept telling me over and over that he had a little money saved up and would move if he could find a nicer convalescent center. He emphasized that there is nothing wrong with his mind, and he does not like being "cooped up" with a lot of crazy people. He asked me to buy him some stamps so that he could write to a lawyer in the city and see if he could get out of there. I asked the registered nurse and the administrator if I could buy the stamps, and they showed concern that he might give me letters to mail without them knowing about it.

I asked the registered nurse why Mr. Adams could not be transferred to a "normal" convalescent center (one not having a license for dealing with mentally disturbed patients). She replied that Mr. Adams is overbearingly crabby and complains continually and that she did not think that he would work out in a "normal" convalescent center.

Mr. Adams is confined to a wheelchair due to polio, but he

can walk a little if he holds on to his wheelchair. He used to work in the valley, dealing with fruits and vegetables. He liked to drink, and one day was found in his cabin more dead than alive from overdrinking. He was taken to the hospital and from there he was moved to the convalescent center.

Mr. Adams is a great baseball fan and spends most of his time reading the sports page and listening to games on his radio. He also likes to talk very much to the staff (not to other patients). He stops whomever he can and begins to talk about baseball. I was his favorite "target," being a man and hence supposedly knowing more about baseball than the aides (all women). One day I decided to take Mr. Adams to a ball game, however, the administrator was very cold about it. She said that Mr. Adams was too excitable and that after all, I was not a relative, and it would have been hard to obtain permission, and the responsibility was too great, and so on until I gave up the idea.

Mr. Adams is very bitter about the center. He feels that the owners take advantage of the patients (such as keeping money allocated for buying new clothing for the patients, and using instead clothing of recently dead patients). He does not like to share a room and the fact that the place is centrally heated and he has no control over regulating the temperature bothers him. He resents the high degree of control that the administrator has over the place, and on various occasions he has had arguments with her.

The regularity with which the "better" patients view themselves as prisoners seems to indicate that believing that they are being held by some conspiracy in a place in which they do not belong allows these individuals to reconcile themselves with their being at the center. Even Mr. Adams' claims to be trying to move are largely rhetorical. I have been in and out of the center for three years now, and he still makes the same claims about leaving, and calling a lawyer, and so on. But as long as the "better" patients view themselves as prisoners, they can survive in the center: The other people here are not their equals, and the staff's treatment is a part of the conspiracy to keep them here.

These are the only individuals who can still view their lives in cognitively meaningful terms. Their lives become seen as a sequence of scheduled events with large gaps of time to be filled in between. One cannot speak of leisure in a setting such as this, a setting which cannot be left freely. The "waiting periods" between scheduled events are filled with activities such as reading, sewing, listening to the radio, etc. These tasks become paramount because they are the only tasks that the patients can themselves choose and regulate to a certain extent. Due to this, a curious thing happens: Leisure becomes equated with sustenance activities, reversing definitions which separate the two.[27] The patients look forward to lunch, to dinner, to their monthly haircut, etc. as the most entertaining events in their lives. The remainder of the time, the "free" time, which should be their leisure time, becomes mere filler, and activities are only useful to "kill time" until the next scheduled events will break the monotony of waiting.

The Others

There are other patients at the center who hang on to a remainder of self. It is often impossible to know how much lucidity they retain because it is hard to crack the solid wall that these patients have erected between themselves and the institution. At times, only at times, a crack appears and one can catch a glimpse of life beneath the dull outside.

I was able to follow the case of a patient before she had set in place the last brick that would forever entomb her alive inside the wall. Mrs. Leister had come to the center willingly because she had a heart condition and felt that she would want medical care nearby all the time. When she came in, she was an active and talkative lady. She walked up and down the corridors, talked to people, smiled a lot and chirpily moved about. One day she was very excited because her daughter was coming to visit her from back East. She showed me a picture of her daughter and told me all about her daughter's husband and children. That very day I witnessed the kind of interaction that was to force Mrs. Leister behind her wall.

The aide came into the room without knocking and left the door opened behind her. Mrs. Leister was fully dressed, but she was lying on the bed awaiting her doctor's visit. The aide, taking no notice of either of us, began making the bed around Mrs. Leister. The doctor walked in and nodded good morning to the aide. He had no way of knowing who I was since he had never met me before, thus I was a stranger of the opposite sex of the patient he was examining; nevertheless, he casually unbuttoned Mrs. Leister's blouse while asking her about her health and began listening with a stethoscope to her heart. He left after a few minutes, and the nurse resumed making the bed while telling me what a terrible doctor that was.

That day Mrs. Leister had her first taste of what it is like to be treated as an object. When she attempted to be a human being, she was met by the unyielding iron hand of regulations. No, she could not go outside the center and take walks, that was against regulations; no, she could not watch television in the evenings, that would disturb the other patients, and it was not allowed; no, there was no portion of the six acres around the center that was set aside for gardening by the patients. Other patients spoke curtly to Mrs. Leister or returned her conversation with an idiotic grin. Old Maria, in her ramblings, once more reverted to the language of her youth when she was a prostitute in the streets of New York, and invested Mrs. Leister with a barrage of profanities, which brought laughter and a thorazine shot from the "battle axe" on duty.

Four months later, Mrs. Leister was spending all of her time on her bed. She no longer walked up and down the corridors. "I can look at the sky from here," she told me, perhaps in her last attempt to have something of her own.

Others who have been at the center longer have finished their wall and devised small ways to show that the center is an abhorrent entity outside of themselves. This enables them to keep a distance between themselves and the center. Goffman observed these behaviors on the part of patients in his work *Asylums* and called them secondary adjustments:

Secondary adjustments provide the inmate with important evidence that he is still his own man, with some control of his environment; sometimes a secondary adjustment becomes almost a kind of lodgment for the self, a *churinga* in which the soul is felt to reside.[28]

The following show some of the small ways in which secondary adjustments emerge at the center.

Old Mr. Walters used to roll his wheelchair back and forth, while banging continuously on the wall with his fist. He did not speak apart from yelling his head off when his pants were wet with his own urine. At Christmas one of the aides brought in a tom-tom to redress Mr. Walter's banging. Mr. Walters, upon receiving his "gift," suddenly looked very somber, then he threw it aside in disgust and began weeping. A senile old man? Maybe.

Mr. Jackson wheeled around his chair mumbling discontent to any and all and expectorated on the floor whenever and wherever he felt like it. Moved by my research instinct, and by the fact that I had to clean the floors, I tried to befriend Mr. Jackson. I began helping him around with his wheelchair whenever he needed help; I tried to carry on small talk while cleaning his room; I turned old tomato cans into spittoons and moved them near him wherever he was. It took me many weeks, but Mr. Jackson began replying to my small talk and he began using the spittoon. But I had to leave, and when I came back the next summer, Mr. Jackson was still there, back to silently spitting on the floor.

Benny Barons had been a good musician. He used to play the saw with a famous band in the 1930s and 1940s. He now sat gloomily and scowled at the world. One of the assistant cooks brought out a checker set and placed it on the table in front of Benny and with no words being exchanged, a checker game began. The cook was slightly ahead in the game when culinary duties called. I took over the game and tried to talk to Benny, with no response. No one else was in the dining hall at the time so we played in silence for a while. Benny would not answer when asked, "Is it my move?" but would not move if it was not his turn. After a while, I purposely made an obvious mistake, and Benny won the game while I was complaining about my stupidity. Again no response. I left him and mentioned the strangeness of the game to the registered nurse, who feigned surprise that he would be capable of playing at all. She told me that he never speaks; he just sits and frowns.

And the rest of the patients? They are shadows who no longer possess a cognitive self. They wander aimlessly through the corridors or sit whimpering in a wheelchair, or groan as their bed sores grow redder. When one displays a spark and begins to rage against a ghost from the past which torments him, another pill is popped in his mouth. Slowly, the eyes turn glassy again and, as order and discipline are restored, the patient, a babbling idiot once more, slowly shuffles away.

Growing Old in an Institution

Earlier in this chapter a summary of interactionist theory in relation to the aged was introduced. It can now be reviewed in light of the data presented. The theory relies basically on four points. Self-image is derived through interaction with others; self-image changes in response to others; cultural values and meanings largely determine how one grows old; environment is an important variable in determining how one ages.

In attempts to interact at the center, a new patient is confronted with other patients and staff. Some patients withdraw within themselves and present a cold, often hostile front toward other patients, as in the cases of Mr. Adams and Mr. Anderson. The remainder are not able to interact competently. A new patient then turns to the staff for interactional purposes. But it has been shown that the staff is too busy accomplishing their daily tasks to stop and consider the patients as human beings. Being treated either as a work object by the staff or as nonexistent by other patients does little to sustain one's conception of wholesomeness. Previous values are shattered and meanings vanish in this environment where the world can only be seen through locked doors and the distorting bluish tint of a picture window.

In attempting to understand why patients present such a

hostile front to others rather than unite and share the burden of their destiny, an analogy must be drawn. Seymour Martin Lipset and his associates[29] in studying the typesetters union discovered that typesetters fraternized with other typesetters in their off-duty activities. Lipset and the others attributed this to a problem of perceived status versus accorded status.

A group feels that it belongs to a certain status category and, therefore, believes that it should be its right to interact with groups in the same status bracket. However, the rest of society accords the group a status inferior to that which it itself perceives. The group is, in other words, rejected by others who feel superior to it and, in turn, rejects groups which it perceives as inferior.

In the center, a single patient can be considered the equivalent of the whole group of typesetters. The patient feels that he belongs to a certain status: being sane, and attempts to interact with individuals whom he considers sane: doctors, nurses, aides, janitors, etc. But they perceive the patient as belonging to an inferior status: work-object, insane, senile, etc., and refuse to interact with him. On the other hand, the patient perceives the other patients as inferior because he assumes them to be bona fide patients deserving of being in the center and thus refuses to interact with them. The patient has only one group left with which to interact: himself.

Of Time and Walls

Being enclosed within walls has pushed some of the patients to create an imaginary, but just as confining, wall of their own. What happens to the meaning of growing old in this situation? Given the primacy of the daily schedule, around which life in the center revolves, the patients are left with the utilization of the periods of time between scheduled events. These become waiting periods, as the patients wait for the next meal, wait for the next bath, wait for tomorrow, wait.

The frequent equation of leisure time with free time[30] proves to be wrong in this case. Reading a book, rolling a big ball of string, looking at the sky are no longer meaningful in themselves but only help to shorten the wait between scheduled events which are the stuff of life at the center.

De Grazia speaks of the impossibility of equating leisure, which is a state of mind, with free time, which is a temporal dimension.[31] But time can be a state of mind, too. The patients seem to consider two kinds of time:[32] the man-made "outer" time comprising clock time, meal time, going-to-bed time, days, months, years, the physiological growing old, the other events of our lives. They also consider "inner" time, the period which they have to themselves between scheduled events of "outer" time. This kind of time is experienced subjectively and can be called "waiting." Waiting is created by the fact that "inner" times are experienced by the individuals contemporaneously but without a direct and equal relation to each other. Hence, one can speak of the right time for doing things in the "outer" time structure, but inner time is one's own time; it goes on independently of the outer events for which one is waiting; it depends upon the meaning one imputes to it.

Ironically, the time one may call one's own, which transcends the boundary of clocked time, does not lead to meaningful leisure pursuits at the center. It leads to boredom and acquires meaning only insofar as it shortens the wait between the outer events from which it is supposedly free.

The outer events scheduled by the staff are the only markers that break up the flow of waiting for the patients. The only meaning of their lives at this stage is to go from one marker to the next in such a way that the waiting period seems to be shortened. Free time has become a curse for the patients, who in their plight remind us of Pozzo in *Waiting for Godot:*

> Have you done tormenting me with your accursed time! ... One day, is that not enough for you, one day he went dumb, one day I went blind, one day we'll go deaf, one day we were born, one day we shall die, the same day, the same second ... they give birth a-stride of a grave, the light gleams an instant, then it is night once more.[33]

NOTES

1. Erving Goffman, op. cit.

2. For a detailed account of patients in hospitals in terms of time and work, see Barney Glaser and Anselm Strauss, *Awareness of Dying.* Chicago: Aldine, 1965; *Time for Dying.* Chicago: Aldine, 1968; and *Anguish.* Mill Valley, Ca.: Sociology Press, 1970.

3. For a detailed ethnography of a convalescent center, see Jaber F. Gubrium, *Living and Dying at Murray Manor.* New York: St. Martin's Press, 1975.

4. Matilda W. Riley and Anne Foner, *Aging and Society,* Vol. 1, Chapter 25, op. cit.

5. Claire Townsend, *Old Age: The Last Segregation,* op. cit.; Mary Adelaide Mendelson, *Tender Loving Greed.* New York: Alfred A. Knopf, 1974.

6. Less than 5 percent of the people over sixty-five years of age in the United States are institutionalized. See *Social and Economic Characteristics of the Older Populations 1974,* U.S. Department of Commerce, Bureau of the Census. Washington, D.C.: U.S. Government Printing Office, 1975.

7. See especially George H. Mead, *Mind, Self and Society.* Chicago: Univ. of Chicago Press, 1934.

8. Herbert Blumer, *Symbolic Interactionism: Perspective and Method.* Englewood Cliffs, N.J.: Prentice-Hall, 1969.

9. See, for instance, Ruth S. Cavan, "Self and Role in Adjustment During Old Age," *Human Behavior and Social Processes,* Arnold Rose, ed. Boston, Mass.: Houghton Mifflin, 1962: 526-536.

10. Arnold M. Rose, "The Mental Health of Normal Older Persons," *Geriatrics* 16 (1961): 459-464; "The Subculture of the Aging, a Topic for Sociological Research," op. cit.; "A Current Theoretical Issue in Social Gerontology," *Middle Age and Aging,* op. cit.

11. Carol L. Estes, op. cit.

12. Arnold Rose, "A Current Theoretical Issue in Social Gerontology," op. cit.; also, see the discussion of growing old earlier in this work.

13. For example, see the joiners and the do-gooders in Chapter 4.

14. Howard S. Becker, "Personal Change in Adult Life," *Sociometry* 27 (1964): 40-53.

15. Erving Goffman, *Asylums.* Garden City, N.Y.: Anchor, 1961.

16. Peter Townsend, "The Purpose of the Institution," *Social and Psychological Aspects of Aging,* Tibbitts and Donahue, eds. New York: Columbia University Press, 1962: 378-400.

17. Peter Weiss, *Marat/Sade.* New York: Pocket Books, 1965.

18. However, I had access to all the medical records of the patients.

19. Lewis Carroll, op. cit., p. 63.

20. In the latter part of my research an increasing number of young mental patients began replacing the old ones in the upper ward. At times I was mistaken by a new aide or a delivery man for a patient because I did not wear a white coat and wandered around the facilities.

21. Barney Glaser and Anselm Strauss, *Anguish,* op. cit.

22. This quote and the remainder in the chapter, unless otherwise noted, are from my field notes taken in the summer of 1974.

23. There are four aides on day shift (7:00 to 3:30), two per wing on each ward, plus two 9:00 aides (9:00 to 5:00).

24. The aide is an older lady in her sixties; she has been at the center for many years and somehow feels responsible for all that goes on in there. This leads her to become easily excitable, as I had the opportunity to witness many times.

25. See, for instance, Abraham Blumberg, *Criminal Justice*. Chicago: Quadrangle, 1967.

26. P. G. Wodehouse, quoted in George Orwell, "In Defense of P. G. Wodehouse," in *The Orwell Reader*. New York: Harcourt Brace & World, 1949: 316.

27. See Chapter 3.

28. Erving Goffman, *Asylums*, op. cit., p. 55.

29. S. M. Lipset, Martin Trow, and James Coleman, *Union Democracy*, op. cit.

30. See the discussion of leisure and free time in Chapter 3.

31. Sebastian de Grazia, op. cit.

32. Inner time is Henry Bergson's *"durée."* See Alfred Schutz, *Reflections on the Problem of Relevance*. New Haven, Conn.: Yale University Press, 1970.

33. Samuel Beckett, op. cit.

Chapter 7

CONCLUSION

Helena: Our remedies oft in ourselves do lie
Which we ascribe to heaven: the fated sky
Gives us free scope; only doth backward pull
Our slow designs when we ourselves are dull.[1]

Nearing the end of this work on the elderly, one is faced with various ideas emerging from the data. These ideas are on different levels; therefore, before pulling together various strings, the kinds of conclusions this work attempts to draw must be clarified.

The question raised in the beginning concerned the meaning of growing old for the elderly. At this point, that meaning can be examined in three different ways. First, Chapters 4, 5, and 6 studied various elders in different settings and examined their daily activities. Thus, the first kind of answer to the meaning of old age can be given in terms of the daily pursuits in which the elderly engage. Second, since the old people studied were questioned in regard to their own notions of what it meant to grow old, the second kind of answer can be given in terms of the meaning of old age as viewed by the elderly. Third, by relying on the findings gathered by first-hand examination of the elderly, the existing theories on the aged can be reviewed and relations between leisure and growing old suggested.

Old Age Seen Through Daily Pursuits

In this work some of the complex ways of growing old have been shown. Rather than growing old in a single fashion, individuals do so in many different ways, thus accounting for a variety of types of old people. It is important to note that this work began by showing the cultural notions about old age and leisure which permeate the members of American society. Having done so, the researcher proceeded to examine how the cultural meanings attributed to old age affected the daily situations of the elderly. The types derived are by no means all inclusive, as there are undoubtedly elders who escaped me. Furthermore, the types derived clearly do not have absolute boundaries between them because many elderly may cross the borders, from, let us say, do-gooders to relaxers, in certain situations of their lives. But what emerges without any doubt is the fact that the cultural outlook of various elders deeply affects their views on old age and thrusts their pursuits in different directions depending on where they fit on the social scale.

De Grazia bleakly stated that leisure is not possible in America since Americans have become enslaved by clocked time and their lives ruled by schedules.[2] Leisure proper, according to de Grazia, cannot be time-bound, thus, he argues, at best Americans can strive for free time but not for leisure. The first group examined in this work, the relaxers, have freed themselves from the tyranny of the clock; they have become the modern heirs of the classical notion of leisure by calmly sipping life out of the cup of their golden years.

The individuals in this group view old age as the time of their lives in which to relax, to do things they always wanted to do. Social ties are loosened and social constraints are minimal for this group. Having enjoyed a successful past, these individuals are not burdened by the remorse of what could have been and never was, nor do they regret the loss of roles productive to society. They go fishing, read books, watch television, play golf, take walks, talk to people, visit museums, with no concern either about being useful or being formally engaged in group activities.

The next group considered was the do-gooders. This group, too, is an example of successful adjustment to old age, but the cultural outlook that leads the do-gooders to success is totally different from that of the relaxers. The individuals in this group are the heirs of the work ethic. Meaning throughout life has been furnished by work and work roles for these individuals and they strive to continue maintaining identification with activities and roles which closely resemble work. They engage in unpaid volunteer activities to help other elders. Thus, they are able to fulfill an instrumental service to society as well as being able to play a role within an organization. The do-gooders find meaning in being dance coordinators, librarians, typists, in delivering meals to other less fortunate elders, in helping them prepare their income tax, in planning their trips, and in many other activities formally organized in a myriad of programs.

The individuals in the next group, the joiners, are often the recipients of the planning done by the do-gooders. These individuals have been called a compromise of classical and work ethics.[3] Work itself has stepped aside at this stage of their lives. The joiners do not regret this; they want to enjoy themselves, to have fun. But an uneasiness lingers deep down in the pit of their stomachs. These individuals have busied themselves all their lives and activity has become synonymous with success.[4] Thus, even now, in their old age they find solace in keeping active since to be active is to be successful. Therefore, joiners tend to feel that the more activities they engage in the more successful they will be. Often this leads to "number counting." The meaning of old age is not in the content of what is done but in the number of things done. Joiners do not speak of the beauty of waltzing in a glittering gown; they do not speak of the sunrise over the Alps which they saw last year; they do not mention the warmth of people they meet at the club. Instead, they enumerate the trips taken in the last few years; they vaunt of the many clubs they belong to; they boast of how busy they are.

The next group examined, the waiters, comprises different subgroups. In dealing with this group, cultural beliefs of leisure are largely irrelevant because other elements override notions of leisure with much more powerful immediacy. The first subgroup, the waiters in crisis, have reached a stage of abandon due to a profound life crisis, which has sapped their will to continue a meaningful existence or even to attempt to find surrogate meaning in activities aimed at filling time. These individuals wander about as spectral souls in a Dantesque Inferno.

The crisis which has striken the other three subgroups walks in rugged clothes—poverty. The sitters, whether restricted by crippling illnesses or just kept glued to a chair for lack of anything better to do, are destitute. They "get by" on about $200 a month and fill their days with small tasks which fend off the boredom and the despair of knowing that there is nothing left. The drifters choose a different way to keep boredom and despair at bay. They move on trying to keep one step ahead of the emptiness of their lives; lost pioneers of a frontier, old age, which for them is nothing but a wasteland. The waiting-for-God group, too, engage in small tasks to pass the days, but how different the prospect! The individuals in this group are walking the wasteland of old age toward an oasis, the afterlife. Thus, whatever calamity life has in store for them can be endured with a smile; no matter how trivial the ways in which they fill their days there will be something better at the end.

Apart from the three subgroups mentioned, other waiters have been seen, the prisoners found in convalescent centers. They are no different from the sitters, apart from the lack of choice to get up and go out. Small activities allow them to pass the time. Sewing on buttons, taking a bath, or eating lunch, have become for them the stuff of life, a life which has become confined between the walls of an institution.

It can be stated, in concluding, that in examining growing old through studying what the elders do, one is faced not so much with the inevitability of growing old, but with the enormous differences in what growing old can mean to different people and how these meanings regulate the elders' lives and can lead to happiness, despair, or just apathy.

Growing Old as Seen by the Members

One of the ways in which I attempted to reach the meaning of growing old was to ask old people themselves. As the text has already shown, most elderly individuals in fact denied that they themselves were old, but gave reasons as to what made "the others" old. Strikingly, the reasons tended to be very uniform. To be old, according to the elderly themselves, means to be conscious of one's ailments, to pity oneself, to become passive, to give up on life. Only in rare cases were individuals willing to consider themselves old or to provide detailed examples of the features which made them or their peers old. Some of these specific features were: illness, becoming widowed, lack of sexual interest, or being treated as old by others.

These findings follow the general trend of other studies. It has been seen earlier,[5] that in self-reports of classification as young, middle-aged, or old, the chronological age of 80 had to be passed before over 50 percent of the respondents considered themselves old, which would lead one to believe that there are many 79-year-old "middle-aged" people running around unnoticed.

What is interesting here is that, as Rosow pointed out,[6] the role of "old person" is quite ambiguous. Attempts to provide role prescriptions for old people have been largely at a loss in finding elements which would define old age. Endeavors to define the role by examining the proscriptions of an old person end up reflecting the values of the individuals doing the study rather than actual role boundaries. The ambiguities of identifying what constitutes being old are mirrored in most of the answers to the question: "What makes a person old?"

Rather than pointing to specific do's and don'ts, the elders identified cultural values as the core of old age. The respondents felt that to keep active was to stay young and that to become passive, to relinquish activities and associations was to become old. Thus, one more step in the cultural beliefs of the elderly can be identified: Previously it has been observed that to be successful is equitable with being active, now success equates with activity and activity with youth. Thus, to be successful is to be active and to be active is to be young.

The depth to which activity values pervade American culture is visible when one notices that the do-gooders and the joiners genuflect to the golden god of activity, and that the relaxers and the waiters tend to equate becoming old with passive behavior. Relaxers and waiters consider activity very important. The difference between them and the other groups is that for the relaxers and the waiters activity can take the form of solitary activity while for the do-gooders and the joiners it is associated with organized pursuits in which one engages along with others.

Americans may have succeeded in freeing themselves from the work ethic, but the dying monster has sprung many new heads: activities. Work no longer provides the central identification of life for many, but activities do. Thus, older individuals find new ways to give their lives meaning, by being a bridge player, a canasta-club member, a shuffleboard contestant, going fishing, watching television, writing postcards or walking in the woods. Not only do activities provide meaning, but they are seen as the panacea to cure the plague of old age: to be active is to keep old age at bay.

Leisure and Growing Old

Various theories of growing old have been discussed alongside the data. It has been seen that all of them seem to fit some group of individuals while they fail to explain others. It is not necessary at this point to repeat the findings of the text, it may, however, be helpful to briefly review the successes and shortcomings of the theories in this work.

Disengagement theory found support at the upper and lower strata of the economic scale. Following a pattern discovered long ago by Durkheim,[7] this study of the elders found that the middle strata of the elders in American society are the ones more socially integrated either as joiners or do-gooders. Rich and poor people tend to disengage themselves from society.

However, this disengagement does not always follow the mutual pattern claimed by Cumming. The rich tend to fit this pattern while the poor more often than not are shoved into disengagement by circumstances beyond their control.

Activity theory was a roaring success with the middle classes, especially with the do-gooders who attempted to hang on to middle-age roles and values. But Havighurst's theory was less than applicable to the waiters and failed to explain the relaxers, who willfully chose not to hang on to middle-age roles but to free themselves from social ties in their golden years of retirement.

Life-cycle theory proved too grandiose to be successfully tested, and while some individuals clearly followed a predictable, unchanging pattern throughout their lives, others were caught in situational changes that completely obliterated their previous patterns of life.

Symbolic-interaction theory was strikingly effective in explaining individuals in convalescent centers. It also must be pointed out that this whole study is affected by this theory, since a study of growing old in a particular setting is bound to be affected by the situational surroundings. For some of the individuals examined, however, although situations and other people were undoubtedly important, other factors were more relevant. For instance, disengaged individuals seemed to have little concern for others and to adapt easily to different situations.

Role-loss theory had its ups and downs too. Generally, it is true that in growing old people lose their previous roles; many remain in a quasi-roleless limbo while others strike back and find new roles to wear. For instance, the role of "aged Casanova," is not a carryover from middle-age roles; and some individuals, such as the *seven,* find a prestige in old age that they never possessed in their younger days. Thus, while it is true that often there is a less than smooth transition into the roles of old age, this transition can nevertheless be made successfully.

The problems with the various theories stem from their attempts to explain old age with models which rely on a small

CHART 1

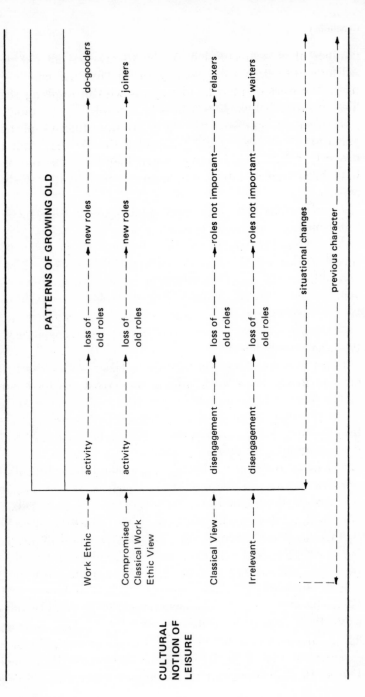

PATTERNS OF GROWING OLD

CULTURAL
NOTION OF
LEISURE

Work Ethic ——	activity ————	loss of —— old roles	————	new roles ————	do-gooders
Compromised Classical Work Ethic View	activity ————	loss of —— old roles	————	new roles ————	joiners
Classical View ——	disengagement ———	loss of —— old roles	————	roles not important———	relaxers
Irrelevant——	disengagement ———	loss of —— old roles	————	roles not important———	waiters

situational changes ————

previous character ————

number of elements. For example, to say that all old people willfully disengage from society or that all old people grasp on to the roles of their middle age, is wishful thinking at best. Simple models in sociology possess a powerful attraction, but, unfortunately, simple models give no more than simplistic explanations.[8] What is more, often the theories have not been properly tested in the field or when they have, the old people have been framed into a preconceived mold that scarcely fits them.

In this study, too, the types derived are not complete descriptions of every old person in American society but use features found in a large number of empirical cases and cluster them in such a fashion as to create ideal types[9] of old people which may aid social scientists in explaining the process of growing old. This is the major contribution of this work to the study of the elderly: the identification of empirically grounded, distinct patterns of growing old. Let us examine how these types have been derived.

Chart 1 views old age in relation to leisure. No serious effort has previously been made among sociologists to look closely at the relation between the two, apart from the work of Kleemeier,[10] which contained an interesting collection of essays but was too loosely structured to provide any real lead toward a general theory of growing old and of leisure.

Let us follow Chart 1 through its various steps. Cultural notions of leisure can be important in four ways in determining types of growing old. Individuals deeply steeped in the work ethic will be attracted to work-like activities in the latter years of their lives and become do-gooders. Other individuals, holding a compromised (classical/work-ethic) view of leisure, will still seek activity but in more leisurely pursuits, and become joiners. Individuals holding a classical view of leisure will no longer be possessed by the continuous need to be busy and will willingly disengage, becoming relaxers. For others, notions of leisure are irrelevant because they are either too poor or have experienced a deep crisis, which has obliterated their previous values. These are the waiters, and they too become disengaged.

Regardless of propensities to disengage or to be active, most individuals face a loss of smooth role transition when they grow old. But their reactions to role losses are not uniform. Those who seek activity will refuse to disengage and quietly blend in with the furniture; they will reengage in new roles. Those who are less constrained by the value of activity will forego new clearly defined roles within organized settings and organizations and engage in solitary pursuits.

While people undergo the transition between middle and old age, situational changes will be extremely important in shaping their future. For example, take any of the individuals examined and place him in the convalescent center studied and there will be a drastic change in his growing old. Also, previous character is always an important factor to be considered in attempting to see how an individual will age.

Chart 1 provides a framework with which to study leisure and old age by incorporating all of the major theories on growing old and by including the meaning of leisure to various individuals. This approach removes the two shortcomings of existing theories: taking-for-granted the meaning of leisure and viewing one's own theory as the only valid one.

There is one more point to be discussed. In examining the types of elders presented in this work, a clearer picture of the relationship between activity and the elders is possible. It has been pointed out and borne out by the data that the meaning attributed to activity varies. Some elders see old age as the chance to do what they always wanted while others are just filling in time. Chart 2 provides a way to understand the relation between types of elderly and the meaning attributed to activities.

Organized refers to activities which take place within a formal organization, providing clear roles and rules of behavior for the members of the organization, for example, working as a volunteer librarian, joining a card club, etc.

Free (or disengaged) indicates activities which have no formal organization, whether undertaken alone or with others, for example, going fishing, taking walks, going out to lunch with friends, etc.

CHART 2

| | | Activity | |
		Organized	Free*
Meaning	Content	Do-gooders	Relaxers
	Form	Joiners	Waiters

*NOTE: Free is taken to mean disengaged, since disengagement does not mean complete cessation of activities, but an involvement with activities which satisfy the self and are detached from social considerations, what Cumming calls "specific-affective" interactional activities. See Elaine Cumming, "Disengagement: A Tentative Theory of Aging," op. cit.

Content denotes a deep attachment to the meaning provided by an activity, regardless of whether the activity is oriented toward others or toward the self, for example, working as a volunteer to help others or reading a book with deep pleasure.

Form points to activities which are not deeply meaningful in themselves but are undertaken because they are ways of passing the time or keeping active.

If the activity is organized and the content is important, the resulting type of elder will be that of a do-gooder. If the activity is organized but the form predominates, the individual will be a joiner. If the activity is free and the content is important, he will be a relaxer, but if the form is more important, his type will be that of a waiter.

The Last Frontier

After some conclusions about the meaning of old age and the possible ways to study it, a few words must be said about what happens to individuals when they become old. Throughout their lives human beings stack a variety of colored blocks and call the resulting pyramid a self. When they cross a certain frontier, called old age, the pyramid becomes very unstable, and a slight push by something or someone sends the blocks and the self tumbling down.

The more one moves toward old age, the more unfamiliar the territory which surrounds one appears and the less likely the individual is to know how to act properly. The routines that regulate one's life disappear; the roles which one acted out dwindle. The last frontier of life is an unknown one; there are no brochures describing what is to come. Thus, just as the frontier tested the true mettle of the pioneers who dared venture into unknown land, so the frontier of old age tests the people who cross it.

Some individuals venture on fearlessly seeking the pastures of their golden years. With no fear or remorse for what they once were, they accept the vagueness of their new state as a blessing. They can go in any direction as there are no clear boundaries to block their path. They are the relaxers. Others fear the uncertainties of the unknown. They are the settlers in this frontier. They make camp; they create new roles and new routines and soon are as busy and as filled with duties and activities as they once were. They are the do-gooders and the joiners. Still others pass this frontier without the proper equipment. They come face to face with the dangers of old age and must bow their heads and suffer, not really having a chance to discover the new frontier but only concerned with surviving. These are the waiters. Finally, some become too weak to care for themselves. The others cannot wait for them; they have become too slow; they are a burden. The weak are corralled into convalescent centers and left behind to die.

NOTES

1. William Shakespeare. *All's Well That Ends Well,* Act I, Scene I.
2. Sebastian de Grazia, op. cit.
3. B. Berger, in Smigel, op. cit.
4. Robert J. Havighurst, op. cit.
5. Jacob Tuckman and Irving Lodge, op. cit.
6. Irving Rosow, *Socialization to Old Age,* op. cit.
7. Emile Durkheim, *Suicide,* op. cit.
8. R. Bendix and B. Berger, op. cit.
9. H. A. Gerth and C. Wright Mills, op. cit.
10. *Aging and Leisure,* Robert W. Kleemeier, ed. New York: Oxford University Press, 1961.

APPENDIX

I have doubts about the appropriate method for discussing methods.[1]

The purpose of this appendix is not to provide a comprehensive account of problems[2] and strategies[3] of field research. After many years during which problems of research were closely guarded,[4] along with the understanding of the relevance of the problematic features of research[5] came the need to unburden oneself of problems encountered in the field. Thus, reading a methodological appendix often became like reading the memoirs from the confessional of a Catholic priest. Problems, incongruencies, peccadilloes, and doubts all came out in a catharsis.[6] Various methodological appendices made interesting reading in their own right.[7] The aim of this appendix is neither cathartic nor programmatic but rather an attempt to clarify the choice of a method, participant observation with open-ended interviews,[8] to explicate the theoretical implications which led to the use of such method, to unveil the often overlooked assumptions present in the use of a particular method, and to present some of the problems encountered by the researcher in the various settings.

Methodology and Paradigms

The decision to choose a particular methodology often runs deeper than the simple choice of a particular tool for a certain job. It entails subscribing to a particular paradigm. Thomas S. Kuhn, in his seminal work *The Structure of Scientific Revolutions*,[9] points to the importance of paradigms. By this term, Kuhn means an achievement with two characteristics:

> Their achievement was sufficiently unprecedented to attract an enduring group of adherents away from competing modes of scientific activity. Simultaneously, it was sufficiently open-ended to leave all sorts of problems for the redefined group of practitioners to resolve.[10]

Examples of a paradigm could be "Ptolemaic astronomy" or "Newtonian dynamics." In following a particular paradigm one engages in the undertakings of "normal science": "Research firmly based upon one or more past scientific achievements, achievements that some particular scientific community acknowledges for a time as supplying the foundation for its further practise."[11] The scientific endeavor transcends the logical aspects of the enterprise since the scientist is tied to the community with which he shares a paradigm in terms of resources, culture, loyalties, etc. Individuals carry out "normal science" within a group which shares the same general beliefs about the science in question. Thus, within a particular paradigm there exists a general consensus about the model to employ. This model need not be explicitly invoked in each study but can be tacitly assumed as the hidden ground rules of one's work.

A perfect example that methodological choice depends upon the tacit assumption of a paradigm is furnished by Bernard Meltzer and John Petras in their essay "The Chicago and Iowa Schools of Symbolic Interactionism."[12] George H. Mead's inspirational theories about the self[13] were approached in entirely different empirical fashions by the "Chicagoans" led by Herbert Blumer and by the "Iowans" led by the late Manford H. Kuhn. Kuhn, relying upon a positive paradigm, approached the study of the self in an "objective" fashion and sought to elucidate its nature by empirical testing which would be analyzed by a scaling system. Blumer and his students on the other hand were committed to a humanistic paradigm. They sought to examine man in his natural setting, the everyday world, and to understand the meaning imputed by social actors to their world. This fundamental difference led Blumer and Kuhn to view the self in entirely different ways:

> While Blumer's image of man dictates his methodology, Kuhn's methodology dictates his image of man. Thus, Blumer begins with a depiction of man's behavior . . . in the course of which acts are constructed. . . . Oppositely, Kuhn starts from a scientific concern . . . [which] brings him to an acceptance of a basically deterministic image of behavior.[14]

The above example is intended to clarify the dependency of particular methodologies upon different paradigms rather than to praise or criticize any given approach. On the contrary, it would be ideal to be able to reconcile various paradigmatic approaches in a unified quest for knowledge.[15] However, in this particular study, participant observation and open-ended interviews were chosen because the topic of inquiry is *meaning,* which places this study within a particular paradigm often referred to as "the humanistic perspective."[16]

Not only is the study of meaning a humanistic endeavor, but studying meaning in the everyday activities of a group, the elderly, necessitates close contact with that group, thus the use of participant observation and interviewing.

Participant Observation

When speaking of participant observation there is a tendency to flatten out differences among the different studies using this approach. There are, however, great variations in how people use participant observation. This point has been clearly made by John Johnson,[17] who shows variance ranging from "subjective naturalism," with little concern expressed for the problem of objectivity in social research, all the way to "formalistic naturalism," where, along with a commitment to the study of everyday life, the researcher has an obligation to explicate methodological procedures and theoretical claims.

Becker and Geer define participant observation:

> By participant observation we mean that method in which the observer participates in the daily life of the people under study, either openly in the role of researcher or covertly in some disguised role, observing things that happen, listening to what is said, and questioning people, over some length of time.[18]

The researcher leaves his familiar world armed with only his "skill and sensitivity."[19] He is now faced with practical problems. At first, he must decide what kind of participant observer he wants to be, covert or overt,[20] full participant, observer, or somewhere in between; the researcher also has to consider the limitations imposed by the setting.[21]

Depending on the researcher's choice he will act in different ways. The choice of becoming either an "active" or a "passive"[22] observer is based on the importance of interacting (or not interacting) with the studied group. The advantage claimed by supporters of the "active" approach is basically that they reach a better understanding of the group by sharing its way of life. The spokesmen for the "passive" approach claim more objectivity because of their detachment and noninterference with the group.

Researchers subscribing to participant observation often go through painstaking efforts to outline the extent to which they became involved. The researcher in his involvement in the situation becomes himself a topic to be studied. It is very hard to be the "studier" and the "studied" at the same time, and one risks becoming so reflexively involved with one's own part in the interaction that one fails to see the interaction itself.[23] If the researcher were to fail, he would no longer be a sociologist but would resemble a flamenco dancer, who, in the words of Lenny Bruce, is "a guy who's always trying to get a look at his own ass."[24]

I often found the dilemma between observation and participation to be not an abstract choice made in a detached and scientific way, but something which overwhelmed me and swept me along with the course of events. An example will clarify the point. One day while doing research at the convalescent center, I was talking to one of the aides while she was beginning to change the bedding of one of the patients who had urinated and soaked the bed. He was the old, blind, ex-wrestler confined in the emergency room.[25] Suddenly, the wrestler decided he was not going to cooperate with the aide and began striking violently at the air about him, fortunately missing the aide. Since nobody else was around, I had no choice but to hold the patient pinned down to the bed while the aide proceeded to change the bedding. It was not pleasant: The patient was squirming and yelling horrible threats at the top of his voice; the acid smell of urine was nauseating; I was slowly loosing my grip on the much stronger patient, while all along feeling horribly like Chief Bromden when he suffocates the lobotomized Mac Murphy in Ken Kesey's novel.[26] But there was no choice, one just could not sit back and take notes while the patient tore apart the aide.

Accessing the Setting

The participant observer must gain access to the setting he wants to study in order to proceed with the research. The techniques for doing so are varied, partly depending on whether one has decided to conduct overt or covert research. The problems encountered in gaining entrée are innumerable, and many accounts of them are to be found in the literature.[27] Entrée is not a *one-time deal* but is continually negotiable and revokable throughout the study. The researcher, whatever technique he may be using, "playing both sides against the middle"[28] or "being a nice guy,"[29] is trying to "get in," which is a sine qua non for the whole research project.

Different settings and different individuals are open to different strategies and present different problems. In studying an organized setting one may choose to approach the administrators of the organization. In this study I dealt with two organizations: the Sunny Hill Convalescent Center and the Corbett Senior Citizen Center. The problems of entrée were entirely different. At the Corbett Center, the director was a student and a good friend of mine and entrée proved to be completely problem free. Having accessed the center, I had to negotiate my entrée individually with each elder I interviewed, but although this presented problems, being rejected by an individual was a minimal setback compared to the crucial issue of access to the center itself. At times, research actually became a field research-er's dream and at times events became rather comfortable, especially when a subject drove me to her home in her Mercedes and fed me homemade cookies while being interviewed.

It was a different matter at the convalescent center. My first stint there was in the guise of a janitor, and the administrator alone was aware that the janitor/researcher might use some information for a school paper. The following year, when I returned to the center, the administrator was very happy to allow an ex-staff member to study the place, in the obvious hope that the researcher would "understand" the organizational problems that governed the events within the center. However, the ownership of the convalescent center had changed hands in the meantime. Thus, while entrée was existing with the ad-ministrator and the nurses, it had to be regained with the owner (the few patients who bothered to ask were told that I was doing some volunteer social work).

The owner reacted to my request to study the place in a strange way. At first he attempted to use my "free" services and considered firing the social worker and have me fill out the reports on the patients. After I explained to him that I was not qualified to engage in such a task, his interest in me dwindled.[30] He told me he could not give me official permis-sion to do research at the center since that would entail clearing the way with patients, doctors, families, MediCal, etc. Then he told me that if a photographer were to ask him permission to take a picture of the center, he could not give him permission, but that if the photographer were to be unobtrusive he certainly would make no effort to stop him. I read the owner's message clearly and rephrased my request by asking him if I would be allowed to visit the patients frequently. He smiled and granted me permission. I never saw him again and had clear access to the center, including the medical records of the patients (I never asked to see financial records as I knew full well that that request would have been denied and would have raised suspicion).

Entrée to the poor people downtown proved extremely problematic, since I was not studying a particular setting but people within a fairly wide ecological range. How does one walk into an old hotel and ask for permission to interview the dozens and dozens of old men sitting along the walls? Entrée had to be gained each and every time, and "being a nice guy" was certainly far more successful than any scientific rhetoric I attempted to use.

Two incidents quickly taught me to keep a low profile as a scientist and rely on my personal charm[31] instead. Having entered a senior citizen center in the downtown area to interview some of the elders, I was approached by the social worker in charge since I was obviously too young to be a senior citizen. The social worker reacted favorably to the "scientific rhetoric" presented and said: "Let me introduce you around." My feeling of pleasure at having the chance to meet some of the old people at the center subsided when I realized that my introduction was to be different than I had expected. Entrenched in a schooling of "low profile" research, I suddenly became the embarrassed center of attention as the social worker dragged me up to the middle of the dance floor, stopped the music and introduced me and my purpose to a bemused group of elders.

The next incident occurred a few days later at the same center. I was listening to the conversation between an older unemployed man who was bitterly complaining about age discrimination[32] in employment and an old, weather-worn fellow in a brownish raincoat. I moved next to the two and joined sporadically in the conversation, but mostly listened to their talk. The fellow in the raincoat took frequent trips to the toilet, which, as I realized later, is the convivial place where brown paper bags containing bottles of dubious quality wine are pulled out and imbibition occurs. Anyway, after a few trips and a few swigs of wine the old fellow became quite boisterous.

Sensing trouble I stood up and began to leave when the fellow insistently asked what my job was. I told him that I was a sociologist doing research on the elders. Once more, "low-profile" research went by the wayside. The old fellow stood up and berated me for engaging in a useless pursuit rather than working in a "solid" field such as chemistry. He even yelled out a few formulas to impress me with his "scientific" knowledge. What was I doing in the meantime? I had quickly slunk to a chair in the corner of the room to avoid eye contact with the old fellow and was not replying to any of his invectives. He soon wandered off in a rage as I sat there recounting the advantages of mailed questionnaire techniques.

Gaining Trust

Developing trust is another major problem facing a participant observer who attempts to gain access to the subjects. The researcher needs to establish trust: "When the observed become convinced that the observer's attitude toward them is one of respect and interest in them as human beings as well as research subjects, they will feel less need for concealing, withholding, or distorting data."[33] How does the researcher know when he is trusted? There are various ways to know this, ranging from the use of informants as a check to "getting to see what's behind the scenes for yourself."[34]

In this research the problems of trust varied enormously in the varied settings. The upper-class individuals interviewed understood quite well the nature of the study and had no fears about the researcher. The middle-class individuals tended to be somewhat more suspicious, but once they realized that the interviewer was a "nice young man," they became extremely friendly and began speaking about personal matters in a relaxed way. The problems arose in studying the poor old people in the old hotels downtown. Numerous rejections left me puzzled about my research abilities. At first, I tried "dressing down" to the level of the subjects: shabby trousers and an old shirt. When this apparel did not prove successful, I tried "dressing up": a nice shirt, neat pants, and a new sweater. Again, no success. A few days later, at one of the senior citizen centers downtown, while talking to an old fellow who lived in the very hotel that had been the scene of my debacle, I mentioned my streak of bad luck.

My discussion with the old fellow had been casual; I wasn't even attempting to interview him and did not have a tape recorder (which from then on I often left behind). But serendipity[35] struck again. The old fellow gave me a lecture on presentation of self and the ecological zones of the city.[36] The old hotel I had attempted to study is in the same area as the gambling rooms, along with massage parlors, cheap bars, pawnbrokers, etc. Thus, in that area a young man is automatically suspicious to the old fellows since "con games"[37] and rip-offs are numerous, and the elders are often the butt of these activities. When I "dressed down," the old man said, I was probably taken for a bum trying to "hustle a buck," and when I "dressed up," I probably was taken for a pimp. But a few blocks away, although still in the poor area of town, the danger was no longer present.[38] Thus, many more elders would talk to me in places like the Mission, the Salvation Army, the Senior Citizen Center, the Friendship Club, etc.

Gathering Data

Thus far, the discussion has focused on the ways in which a participant observer decides how to conduct his study; some of the problematic features of entrée and trust have been explored. The real problem, however, has just begun: the gathering of data. This becomes a daily activity for the researcher as he continually comes into contact with observable data in his encounters with the groups studied. Becker and Geer give a clear account of what kind of data is collectible through the use of participant observation: "In short, participant observation makes it possible to check description against fact. . . . We add to the accuracy of our data when we substitute observable facts for inferences. . . . In short, attention can be focused both on what has happened and on what the person says about what has happened."[3][9]

While Becker and Geer are basically right that physical closeness to the interaction allows the researcher to observe factual events, things are not as simple as they appear. Claims such as letting the data speak for themselves[40] or a return to the phenomena[41] overlook the fact that people and events do not carry labels advising the researcher about their importance as data. Rather, what Robert Pirsig says about the assembly of a motorcycle holds true for the social world as well: "The right facts, the ones we really need, are not only passive, they are damned *elusive,* and we're not going to just sit back and 'observe' them. We're going to have to be in there *looking* for them or we're going to be here for a long time. Forever."[42]

The elusiveness of what constituted important data troubled me for months until certain patterns began emerging in the various settings and allowed me to focus more specifically on certain features of the interaction. What to do in the meantime? The literature is full of "how to" advice on note taking in the field. Lofland, among others, provides the readers with painstaking instructions, even considering elements such as the advantages of typing your own field notes versus handwriting them.[43] Unfortunately, often things do not happen in such an organized fashion,[44] and the researcher is confronted by faulty electronic equipment,[45] false leads, odd hours, faulty memory, laziness, poor organization, and, above all, a continuous bewilderment about what to write down in his field notes.

Sometimes data are very intangible. For instance, when I was doing research at the convalescent center as a janitor, I could tell every morning when I entered the center what kind of day it was going to be by the smell of the place. If the first thing that hit me was a strong smell of excrements, invariably it had been a bad night, patients had "caused trouble," and I faced the prospects of unclogging three or four toilets. If the smell of excrements was just a faint trace in the air, the night had been calm, and we could expect a quiet day. Were my olfactory senses important data? And if so, what way?

Having gathered and ordered the data in some meaningful categories, the researcher should check on the reliability of the information at hand. The use of "inside" informants is usually the most reliable way to check out information.[46] The research conducted at the Corbett Senior Citizen Center was easily double-checked since the director herself was my informant. I also knew well a couple of volunteers who had been students in my aging classes at ——— College. In quite a few cases, the inside information revealed facets that I had not been able to uncover through my research. For instance, Mr. Bismark,[47] while never hiding his opulence, certainly did not give me a detailed account of his finances; this information was acquired by me through my informant. At the Sunny Hill Convalescent Center I was my own inside informant the first period of my research. The second time a very close relation of mine was the licensed vocational nurse in charge of the night shift thus enabling me to verify many details. My situation in studying the elders downtown was much more precarious. I had no inside informants and had to rely on "sympathetic old people" to check out my information. Having written a rough draft of my various typologies in different settings, I presented it to many elderly, sometimes individually, other times during seminars on aging (many of my students were elderly or worked with the elderly; for instance, one of them was a recreation director at a convalescent center, another organized a free-food service for a senior center, etc.). My data withstood the "members' test of validity" extremely well.

The Implications of Participant Observation

"I cannot conceive myself as nothing but a bit of the world, a mere object of biological, psychological or sociological investigation. I cannot shut myself up within the realm of science. All my knowledge of the world, even my scientific knowledge, is gained from my particular point of view."[48] Merleau-Ponty's brilliant insight not only questions the subject-object dualism present in the work of his mentor, Edmund Husserl,[49] but introduces a point which is basic in the use of participant observation: The researcher is a part of the world which he seeks to explicate, and the knowledge he acquires stems from his position in this world.

It is important to examine this point since this work tacitly relies on it, just as other field work does. C. Wright Mills called the researcher's ability to understand man in a certain historical time and within a particular culture, the sociological imagination.[50] This ineffable quality is what enables us, as researchers, to extract orderly categories out of the chaotic vortex of raw data. A participant observer assumes a particular role, gauges the distance he will keep and the part he will play in the interaction; he accesses the group and gains the members' trust. In short, the researcher is himself, the instrument by which the data will be gathered, organized and reported.

If the researcher provides the interpretive procedures used to understand a particular section of the world, the implied assumption of participant observation is that the world is only explicable by recreating experiences of others through the sociological imagination of the researcher. Thus, no objective knowledge in any absolute sense can be derived from sociological inquiries but an intersubjective understanding can be reached through empathy with the subjects of the study.

Understanding[51] (verstehen) and the meaning derived through understanding become the most important elements in such an approach to the social sciences. Researchers cannot, as in experimental situations, rely upon a starting point of observation. Rather, they are confronted with a circle[52] of events in which there is no starting point but in which understanding is only possible through a particular viewpoint, thus eliminating presuppositionless knowledge and placing meaning within a particular frame of reference.

The Sociologist as a Writer

Having gathered the data, the sociologist has completed only half of his task; he must now report his findings. Just as in the gathering process, so in the reporting one, data do not speak for themselves. The sociologist is in possession of highly abstract materials; as Alfred Schutz perceptively points out, "the concepts formed by the social scientist are constructs of the constructs formed in common sense thinking by the actors on the social scene."[53] The social scientist, having understood the social scene which was the topic of his inquiry, has to translate his understanding by relying closely on the material gathered, in such a fashion as to allow the readers to emphasize with the study.

Glaser and Strauss consider two steps that must be followed in reporting field data. First, the researcher must make his theoretical framework understandable; second, he must "describe so vividly the social world studied that the reader can almost literally see and hear its people."[54] This work has attempted to follow the two steps pointed out by Glaser and Strauss. Theory has been introduced at the beginning of the study and summarized at the end, but it has also been presented alongside the empirical findings, because in the end the theory depends on the empirical findings themselves. An attempt has also been made to present the study in such a fashion that would vividly set forth the subject matter; this often entailed summarizing interviews, selectively choosing elements which seemed more important, presenting some subjects and leaving many more out, but hopefully, the result has been to give a live picture of the events rather than pages and pages of garbled transcripts analyzed in an unintelligible language.

Unfortunately, many sociologists have been for too long under the yoke of obscure Parsonian prose, as so aptly shown by C. Wright Mills,[55] and social messages are often suffocated in obtuse language. But if the sociologists hope, and some of us do, in the wake of the great Max Weber, to demystify the world and present its social members with analytic insights about the invisible webs[56] that hold it together, it is not enough to simply see the world stripped of its veils. Sociologists must strip their own language of the veils which hide their revelations from the members of society and present their sociological understanding with a new kind of sociological imagination, one that will guide the sociologist's pen to paint a portrait of society which will stir empathy and understanding among readers. Until this new imagination is found, one can say of many contemporary sociologists what Nietzsche said of the German writers of his time: "They all are nothing more than veil-makers (Schleiermacher)."[57]

NOTES

1. Melville Dalton, "Preconceptions and Methods in Men Who Manage," *Sociologists at Work,* Phillip E. Hammond, ed. Garden City, N.Y.: Anchor, 1967: 58.

2. For a brilliant exposition of problems in the field, see John Johnson, *Doing Field Work.* New York: Free Press, 1976.

3. For a comprehensive and insightful approach to field strategies, see Jack D. Douglas, *Investigative Social Research: Individual and Team Field Research.* Beverly Hills: Sage, 1976.

4. For a revealing account, see Murray Wax, "Tenting with Malinowski," *American Sociological Review* 37 (1972): 1-13.

5. See Aaron Cicourel, *Method and Measurement in Sociology.* New York: Free Press, 1964.

6. See, among others, Rosalie Wax, "Twelve Years Later: An Analysis of a Field Experience," *American Journal of Sociology* 63 (1957): 133-142, for the problem of doing research while drinking saki; John Johnson, op. cit., for the problem of becoming emotionally involved to the point of crying, and William F. Whyte, *Street Corner Society,* Chicago: University of Chicago Press, second edition, 1955, for the problem of breaking the law to maintain trust.

7. Phillip Hammond, ed., op. cit.

8. Some researchers consider the use of participant observation and that of interviews as separate methodologies, see for instance the classic statement by Howard Becker and Blanche Geer, "Participant Observation and Interviewing: A Comparison," *Human Observation* 16 (1957): 28-52. Others come closer to the approach taken in this work and consider the two as complementary. See Norman Denzin, *The Research Act.* Chicago: Aldine, 1970.

9. Thomas S. Kuhn, op. cit.

10. Ibid., p. 10.

11. Ibid., p. 10.

12. *Human Nature and Collective Behavior. Papers in Honor of Herbert Blumer,* T. Shibutani, ed. Englewood Cliffs, N.J.: Prentice-Hall, 1970.

13. See especially George H. Mead, *Mind, Self, and Society,* op. cit.

14. Ibid., p. 14.

15. See Norman Denzin, op. cit., for a similar approach. Denzin invokes the use of "triangulation," i.e., relying on different methodologies in sociological studies.

Bennett Berger once suggested, in personal conversation, that it would be ideal to be able to make quantitative statements about society but unfortunately this is not possible in many instances thus forcing us to rely upon different procedures.

16. Severyn T. Bruyn, *The Humanistic Perspective in Sociology.* Englewood Cliffs, N.J.: Prentice-Hall, 1966.

17. John Johnson, op. cit.

18. Howard S. Becker and Blanche Geer, op. cit., p. 28.

19. Ibid., p. 29.

20. Jack D. Douglas, "Observing Deviance," *Research on Deviance,* Jack D. Douglas, ed. New York: Random House, 1972.

21. Morris Schwarts and C. Schwartz, "Problems of Participant Observation," *American Journal of Sociology* 60 (1955): 343-353.

22. Ibid., p. 348.

23. See, for instance, the solipsistic work of Alan Blum, "Theorizing," *Understanding Everyday Life,* Jack D. Douglas, ed., op. cit.

24. Albert Goldman, *Ladies and Gentlemen, Lenny Bruce!!* New York: Ballantine, 1971: 284.

25. See Chapter 6.

26. Ken Kesey, *One Flew Over the Cuckoo's Nest.* New York: Signet, 1962.

27. See, especially, John Johnson, op. cit.

28. Ibid.

29. John Lofland, *Analyzing Social Settings.* Belmont, CA.: Wadsworth, 1971.

30. See Joseph R. Gusfield, "Field Work Reciprocities in Studying a Social Movement," *Human Organization* 14 (1955): 29-34, for the notion of "what's in it for me?" in field research.

31. See John Johnson, op. cit.

32. Erdman B. Palmore and Kenneth Manton, "Ageism Compared to Racism and Sexism," op. cit.

33. Morris Schwartz and C. Schwartz, op. cit., p. 347.

34. See, especially, Jack D. Douglas, *Investigative Social Research,* op. cit., for a discussion of "fronts" and trust.

35. Serendipity is: "the discovery by chance of sagacity of valid results which were not sought for." Robert K. Merton, *Social Theory and Social Structure.* New York: Free Press, enlarged edition, 1968: 157.

36. For sociological theories on ecology, see Robert K. Park and Ernest W. Burgess, *The City.* Chicago: University of Chicago Press, 1967.

37. For an interesting article on "con games," see Erving Goffman, "On Cooling the Mark Out: Some Aspects of Adaptation to Failure," *Psychiatry Journal for the Study of Interpersonal Relations* 15 (1952): 451-463.

38. For a study of zones of danger and appearances in the city, see Erving Goffman, *Relations in Public.* New York: Harper and Row, 1971.

39. Howard S. Becker and Blanche Geer, op. cit., pp. 30-32.

40. David Matza, *Becoming Deviant.* Englewood Cliffs, N.J.: Prentice-Hall, 1962.

41. Alfred Schutz, *Collected Papers I,* op. cit.

42. Robert M. Pirsig, *Zen and the Art of Motorcycle Maintenance.* New York: Bantam, 1974: 275.

43. John Lofland, op. cit.

44. For an interesting account of how notes are taken in the field, see the movie *All the President's Men* in which the reporters scribble away on whatever happens to be in front of them at the time.

45. See John Johnson, op. cit., for an account of tape recorder malfunctioning.

46. See Jack D. Douglas, *Investigative Social Research,* op. cit., especially the account of massage parlors for the importance of checking data.

47. See Chapter 4.

48. Maurice Merleau-Ponty, *Phenomenology of Perception.* London: Routledge and Kegan Paul, 1962: viii.

49. See, especially, Edmund Husserl, *Phenomenology and the Crisis of Philosophy.* New York: Harper and Row, 1965.

50. C. Wright Mills, *The Sociological Imagination.* New York: Oxford University Press, 1959.

51. The philosophy of Wilhelm Dilthey. See, for instance, *Patterns and Meaning in History.* New York: Harper and Row, 1961. It was important in influencing Max Weber's sociological notion of understanding. On the other hand, Edmund Husserl reacted strongly against the subjectivity of Dilthey.

52. Often referred to as hermeneutic circle, from Hermes, the Greek god who transformed the messages of the gods into understandable forms for the mortals. See Richard E. Palmer, *Hermeneutics.* Evanston, Ill.: Northwestern University Press, 1969.

53. Alfred Schutz, *Collected Papers I,* op. cit.

54. Barney G. Glaser and Anselm L. Strauss, *Awareness of Dying,* op. cit., p. 290.

55. C. Wright Mills, op. cit.

56. See the work of Georg Simmel, especially *The Sociology of Georg Simmel,* Kurt H. Wolff, ed. New York: Free Press, 1950.

57. Nietzsche was referring to the hermeneutic philosopher Schleiermacher (which means veil-maker). He was also addressing Fichte, Schelling, Schopennauer, Hegel, Kant, and Leibniz. Thus, the sociologists who have been called veil-makers can console themselves for they are in illustrious company. See "Il Caso Wagner: Un problema per musicanti," in *Il Meglio di Federico Nietzsche,* op. cit., p. 748. The translation of this quote from the Italian is mine.

REFERENCES

Anderson, Nels, *The Hobo.* Chicago: University of Chicago Press, 1923.

Arenberg, D., "Changes in Memory with Age," *The Psychology of Adult Development and Aging,* edited by C. Eisdorfer and M. P. Lawton. Washington, D.C.: American Psychological Association, 1973.

Barrett, William, *Irrational Man.* Garden City, N.Y.: Anchor, 1962.

Becker, Howard and Blanche Geer, "Participant Observation and Interviewing: A Comparison," *Human Organization* 16 (1957): 28-52.

Becker, Howard, *Outsiders.* New York: Free Press, 1963.

——— , "Personal Change in Adult Life," *Sociometry* 27 (1964): 40-53.

Beckett, Samuel, *Waiting for Godot.* New York: Grove, 1954.

Bell, Clive, "How to Make a Civilization," *Mass Leisure,* edited by E. Larrabee and R. Meyersohn. Glencoe, Ill.: Free Press, 1960.

Bendix, R. and B. Berger, "Images of Society and Problems of Concept Formation in Sociology," *Symposium on Sociological Theory,* edited by Llewellyn Gross. New York: Harper and Row, 1959.

Berger, Bennett, "The Sociology of Leisure," *Work and Leisure,* edited by Erwin Smigel. New Haven, Conn.: College and University Press, 1963.

——— , "How Long is a Generation?" *Looking for America.* Englewood Cliffs, N.J.: Prentice-Hall, 1971.

Berger, Peter, *A Rumor of Angels.* Garden City, N.Y.: Anchor, 1969.

Blau, Zena Smith, "Changes in Status and Age Identification," *American Sociological Review* 21 (1956): 198-203.

Blum, Alan, "Theorizing," *Understanding Everyday Life,* edited by Jack D. Douglas. Chicago: Aldine, 1970.

Blumberg, Abraham, *Criminal Justice.* Chicago: Quadrangle, 1967.

Blumer, Herbert, *Symbolic Interactionism: Perspective and Method.* Englewood Cliffs, N.J.: Prentice-Hall, 1969.

Bruyn, Severyn T., *The Humanistic Perspective in Sociology.* Englewood Cliffs, N.J.: Prentice-Hall, 1966.

Burgess, Ernest, L. G. Cordy, P. C. Pineo, and R. T. Thornbury, "Occupational Differences in Attitudes toward Aging and Retirement," *Journal of Gerontology* 13 (1958): 203-206.

Burgess, Ernest, "Aging in Western Culture," *Aging in Western Societies,* edited by Ernest Burgess. Chicago: University of Chicago Press, 1960.

Carroll, Lewis, *Alice's Adventures in Wonderland.* New York: Signet, 1960.

Cavan, Ruth, "Self and Role Adjustment During Old Age," *Human Behavior and Social Processes,* edited by Arnold Rose. Boston: Houghton Mifflin, 1962.

Cavan, Sherri, *Liquor License.* Chicago: Aldine, 1966.

Charlesworth, J., *Leisure in America: Blessing or Curse.* Philadelphia: The American Academy of Political and Social Sciences, 1964.

Cicourel, Aaron V., *Method and Measurement in Sociology.* New York: Free Press, 1964.

Coser, Lewis, "Two Methods in Search of a Substance," American Sociological Association Presidential Address, 1975.

Cowgill, Donald and Lowell Holmes, eds., *Aging and Modernization.* New York: Appleton-Century-Crofts, 1972.

Cumming, Elaine, Lois R. Dean, David S. Newell, and Isabel McCaffrey, "Disengagement: A Tentative Theory of Aging," *Sociometry* 23 (1960): 23-35.

Cumming, Elaine and W. E. Henry, *Growing Old: The Process of Disengagement.* New York: Basic Books, 1961.

Cumming, Elaine, "Further Thoughts on the Theory of Disengagement," *International Social Science Journal* 15 (1963): 377-393.

Cummings, E. E., *100 Selected Poems.* New York: Grove, 1954.

Curtin, Sharon, *Nobody Ever Died of Old Age.* Boston: Little, Brown, 1972.

Dalton, Melville, *Men Who Manage.* New York: John Wiley, 1959.

de Grazia, Sebastian, *Of Time, Work, and Leisure.* Garden City, N.Y.: Anchor, 1962.

Dennis, Wayne, "Creative Productivity Between the Ages of 20 and 80 Years," *Middle Age and Aging,* edited by Bernice Neugarten. Chicago: University of Chicago Press, 1968.

Denzin, Norman, *The Research Act.* Chicago: Aldine, 1970.

DHEW, Administration on Aging, Publication No. (OHD/ACA) 74-20005.

– – – , "Income and Poverty in 1972-Advance Report." Publication No. (OHD) 74-20008.

Dilthey, Wilhelm, *Patterns and Meaning in History.* New York: Harper and Row, 1961.

Douglas, Jack D., ed., *Understanding Everyday Life.* Chicago: Aldine, 1970.

– – – , "Observing Deviance," *Research on Deviance,* edited by Jack D. Douglas. New York: Random House, 1972.

– – – , *Investigative Social Research: Individual and Team Field Research.* Beverly Hills: Sage, 1976.

– – – and John Johnson, eds., *Existential Sociology.* New York: Cambridge University Press, 1976.

Dubin, R., "Industrial Workers' World: A Study of 'Central Life Interests' of Industrial Workers," *Work and Leisure,* edited by Erwin Smigel. New Haven, Conn.: College and University PRess, 1963.

Dumazedier, Joffre, *Toward a Society of Leisure.* London: Collier-Macmillan, 1962.

Durkheim, Emile, *Suicide.* New York: Free Press, 1951.

– – – , *The Division of Labor in Society.* New York: Free Press, 1964.

Erickson, Erick H., "Generativity and Ego Integrity," *Middle Age and Aging,* edited by Bernice Neugarten. Chicago: University of Chicago Press, 1968.

Esslin, Martin, *The Theatre of the Absurd.* Garden City, N.Y.: Anchor, 1969.

Estes, Carol L., *Community Planning for the Elderly,* unpublished Ph.D. dissertation. University of California, San Diego, 1972.

Fitzgerald, F. Scott, *The Great Gatsby.* New York: Scribner's, 1925.

——— , "The Diamond as Big as the Ritz," *Babylon Revisited and Other Stories.* New York: Scribner's, 1960.

——— , *The Pat Hobby Stories.* New York: Scribner's, 1970.

Fontana, Andrea and Richard VandeWater, "The Existential Thought of Jean Paul Sartre and Maurice Merleau-Ponty," *Existential Sociology,* edited by Jack D. Douglas and John Johnson. New York: Cambridge University Press, 1976.

Freidson, Eliot, *Profession of Medicine.* New York: Dodd, Mead, 1970.

Garfinkel, Harold, *Studies in Ethnomethodology.* Englewood Cliffs, N.J.: Prentice-Hall, 1967.

Gerstl, J., "Leisure, Taste and Occupational Milieu," *Work and Leisure,* edited by Erwin Smigel. New Haven, Conn.: College and University Press, 1963.

Gerth, H. H. and C. Wright Mills, *From Max Weber: Essays in Sociology.* New York: Oxford University Press, 1964.

Giddens, Anthony, "A Note on the Concept of Play and Leisure," *Sociological Review* 12 (1964): 73-89.

Ginzberg, Raphael, "The Negative Attitude Toward the Elderly," *Geriatrics* 7 (1952): 297-302.

Glaser, Barney G. and Anselm L. Strauss, *Awareness of Dying.* Chicago: Aldine, 1965.

——— , *The Discovery of Grounded Theory.* Chicago: Aldine, 1967.

——— , *Time for Dying.* Chicago: Aldine, 1968.

Goffman, Erving, "On Cooling the Mark Out: Some Aspects of Adaptation to Failure," *Psychiatry Journal for the Study of Interpersonal Relations* 15 (1952): 451-463.

——— , *The Presentation of Self in Everyday Life.* Garden City, N.Y.: Anchor, 1959.

——— , *Asylums.* Garden City, N.Y.: Anchor, 1961.

——— , *Relations in Public.* New York: Harper and Row, 1971.

Goldman, Albert, *Ladies and Gentlemen, Lenny Bruce!!* New York: Ballantine, 1971.

Greenberg, C., "Work and Leisure under Industrialism," *Mass Leisure,* edited by E. Larrabee and R. Meyersohn. Glencoe, Ill.: Free Press, 1960.

Grushin, B., *Problems of Free Time in the U.S.S.R.* A.N.H., 1969.

Gubrium, Jaber F., *Living and Dying at Murray Manor.* New York: St. Martin's Press, 1975.

Guicciardini, Francesco, *The History of Italy and History of Florence.* New York: Twayne, 1964.

Gusfield, Joseph, "Field Work Reciprocities in Studying a Social Movement," *Human Organization* 14 (1955): 29-34.

Guthrie, Woody, *Bound for Glory.* New York: Signet, 1943.

Hall, Edward, *The Hidden Dimension.* Garden City, N.Y.: Anchor, 1966.

Hammond, Phillip E., ed., *Sociologists at Work.* Garden City, N.Y.: Anchor, 1967.

Harrington, Michael, *The Other America.* Baltimore: Penguin, 1962.

Havighurst, Robert J., "Flexibility and the Social Role of the Retired," *American Journal of Sociology* 59 (1953-1954): 309-311.

Hemingway, Ernest, *A Movable Feast*. New York: Scribner's, 1964.

Hochschild, Arlie Russell, *The Unexpected Community*. Englewood Cliffs, N.J.: Prentice-Hall, 1973.

Holy Bible, King James' version. New York: Cambridge University Press.

Hughes, Everett, *Men and Their Work*. Glencoe, Ill.: Free Press, 1958.

Husserl, Edmund, *Phenomenology and the Crisis of Philosophy*. New York: Harper and Row, 1965.

Jacobs, Jerry, *Fun City: An Ethnographic Study of a Retirement Community*. New York: Holt, Rinehart, and Winston, 1974.

--- , *Older Persons and Retirement Communities*. Springfield, Ill.: Charles C Thomas, 1975.

Johnson, John, *Doing Field Research*. New York: Free Press, 1976.

Kando, T. and W. Summers, "The Impact of Work and Leisure," *Pacific Sociological Review* 14 (1971): 310-324.

Kaplan, Max, "The Uses of Leisure," *Handbook of Social Gerontology*, edited by C. Tibbitts. Chicago: University of Chicago Press, 1960.

Kesey, Ken, *One Flew Over the Cuckoo's Nest*. New York: Signet, 1962.

Kleemeier, Robert W., ed., *Aging and Leisure*. New York: Oxford University Press, 1961.

Kuhn, Thomas S., *The Structure of Scientific Revolutions*. Chicago: University of Chicago Press, second edition, 1970.

Larrabee, E. and R. Meyersohn, *Mass Leisure*. Glencoe, Ill.: Free Press, 1960.

Lewis, Oscar, *The Children of Sanchez*. New York: Vintage, 1963.

Lipset, S. M., J. Coleman, and M. Trow, *Union Democracy*. Garden City, N.Y.: Anchor, 1956.

Lipset, S. M., "Elections: The Expression of the Democratic Class Struggle," *Class, Status, and Power*, edited by R. Bendix and S. M. Lipset. New York: Free Press, 1966.

Lofland, John, *Analyzing Social Settings*. Belmont, Calif.: Wadsworth, 1971.

Lopata, Helena Znaniecki, *Widowhood in an American Society*. Cambridge, Mass.: Schenkman, 1973.

Lundberg, G. A., *Leisure—A Suburban Study*. New York: Columbia University Press, 1934.

Lyman, Stanford, "The Race Relation Cycle of Robert E. Park," *Pacific Sociological Review* 11 (1968): 16-28.

--- and Marvin Scott, "Territoriality: A Neglected Sociological Dimension," *A Sociology of the Absurd*. New York: Appleton-Century-Crofts, 1970.

Machiavelli, Niccoló, *The Prince*. London: Oxford University Press, 1960.

Matza, David, *Becoming Deviant*. Englewood Cliffs, N.J.: Prentice-Hall, 1962.

--- , "The Disreputable Poor," *Class, Status, and Power*, edited by R. Bendix and S. M. Lipset. New York: Free Press, 1966.

Maves, Paul, "Aging, Religion, and the Church," *Handbook of Social Gerontology,* edited by C. Tibbitts. Chicago: University of Chicago Press, 1960.

McIver, R., *The Pursuit of Happiness.* New York: Simon and Schuster, 1955.

Mead, George H., *Mind, Self and Society.* Chicago: University of Chicago Press, 1934.

Mead, Margaret, "The Pattern of Leisure in Contemporary America," *Mass Leisure,* edited by E. Larrabee and R. Meyersohn. Glencoe, Ill.: Free Press, 1960.

Mendelson, Mary A., *Tender Loving Greed.* New York: Knopf, 1974.

Merleau-Ponty, Maurice, *Phenomenology of Perception.* London: Routledge and Kegan Paul, 1962.

Merton, Robert K., "Social Structure and Anomie," *American Sociological Review* 3 (1938): 672-682.

——— , *The Student Physician.* Cambridge, Mass.: Harvard University Press, 1957.

——— , "The Role Set: Problems in Sociological Theory," *British Journal of Sociology* 8 (1957): 106-120.

——— , *Social Theory and Social Structure.* New York: Free Press, enlarged edition, 1968.

Mills, C. Wright, *The Sociological Imagination.* New York: Oxford University Press, 1959.

Nader, Ralph, *Old Age: The Last Segregation,* Claire Townsend, project director. New York: Bantam, 1970.

Neugarten, Bernice and J. Moore, "The Changing Age-Status System," *Middle Age and Aging,* edited by Bernice Neugarten. Chicago: University of Chicago Press, 1968.

Neugarten, Bernice, ed., *Middle Age and Aging.* Chicago: University of Chicago Press, 1968.

Nietzsche, Federico, *Il Meglio de F. Nietzsche.* Milano: Longanesi, 1956.

Orwell, George, *The Orwell Reader.* New York: Harcourt Brace & World, 1949.

Palmer, Richard E., *Hermeneutics.* Evanston, Ill.: Northwestern University Press, 1969.

Palmore, Erdman and Kenneth Manton, "Ageism Compared to Racism and Sexism," *Journal of Gerontology* 28 (1973): 363-369.

Palmore, Erdman, *Normal Aging II.* Durham, N.C.: Duke University Press, 1974.

Park, Robert and Ernest W. Burgess, *The City.* Chicago: University of Chicago Press, 1967.

Parker, Stanley, *The Future of Work and Leisure.* New York: Praeger, 1971.

Parsons, Talcott, "Old Age as a Consummatory Phase," *The Gerontologist* 3 (1963): 53-54.

——— and Gerald M. Platt, "Higher Education and Changing Socialization," *Aging and Society. Vol. 3: A Sociology of Age Stratification,* edited by Matilda White Riley, Marylin Johnson, and Anne Foner. New York: Russell Sage, 1972.

Pearson, John Ward, *The 8-Day Week.* New York: Harper & Row, 1973.

Peck, Robert C., "Psychological Development in the Second Half of Life," *Middle Age and Aging,* edited by Bernice Neugarten. Chicago: University of Chicago Press, 1968.

Percy, Charles H., *Growing Old in the Country of the Young.* New York: McGraw-Hill, 1972.

Pieper, Josef, *Leisure the Basis of Culture.* New York: Pantheon, 1964.

Pirsig, Robert M., *Zen and the Art of Motorcycle Maintenance.* New York: Bantum, 1974.

Riesman, David, "Work and Leisure in Post-Industrial Society," *Mass Leisure,* edited by E. Larrabee and R. Meyersohn. Glencoe, Ill.: Free Press, 1960.

——— , *The Lonely Crowd.* New Haven, Conn.: Yale University Press, 1961.

Riley, Matilda and Anne Foner, *Aging and Society. Vol. 1: An Inventory of Research Findings.* New York: Russell Sage, 1968.

Roberts, Kenneth, *Leisure.* London: Longman, 1970.

Rose, Arnold and W. A. Peterson, *Older People and Their Social World.* Philadelphia: F. A. Davis, 1965.

Rose, Arnold, "The Mental Health of Normal Older Persons," *Geriatrics* 16 (1961): 459-464.

——— , "A Current Theoretical Issue in Social Gerontology," *Middle Age and Aging,* edited by Bernice Neugarten. Chicago: University of Chicago Press, 1968.

——— , "The Subculture of the Aging: A Topic for Sociological Research," *Middle Age and Aging,* edited by Bernice Neugarten. Chicago: University of Chicago Press, 1968.

Rosow, Irving, "Old Age: Moral Dilemma of an Affluent Society," *The Gerontologist* 2 (1962): 182-191.

——— , *Social Integration of the Aged.* New York: Free Press, 1967.

——— , *Socialization to Old Age.* Berkeley: University of California Press, 1974.

Rubin, Isadore, *Sexual Life After Sixty.* New York: Signet, 1967.

Schutz, Alfred, *Reflections on the Problem of Relevance.* New Haven, Conn.: Yale University Press, 1970.

——— , *Collected Papers I.* The Hague: Martinus Nijhoff, 1971.

Schwartz, Arthur, "A Transactional View of the Aging Process," *Professional Obligations and Approaches to the Aged,* edited by Arthur Schwartz and Ivan Mensh. Springfield, Ill.: Charles C Thomas, 1974.

Schwartz, Morris and Charlotte Schwartz, "Problems of Participant Observation," *American Journal of Sociology* 60 (1955): 343-353.

Sewell, Elizabeth, *The Field of Nonsense.* London: Chatto and Windus, 1952.

Shakespeare, William, *All's Well That Ends Well.* New York: Oxford University Press, 1969.

——— , *King Lear.* New York: Oxford University Press, 1968.

——— , *The Merchant of Venice.* New York: Oxford University Press, 1969.

Shibutani, T., *Human Nature and Collective Behavior. Papers in Honor of Herbert Blumer.* Englewood Cliffs, N.J.: Prentice-Hall, 1970.

Simmel, Georg, *The Conflict in Modern Culture and Other Essays.* New York: Teachers College Press, 1968.

Simmons, Leo W., *The Role of the Aged in Primitive Societies.* New Haven, Conn.: Yale University Press, 1945.

Slater, Philip, *The Pursuit of Loneliness.* Boston: Beacon, 1970.

Smigel, Erwin, *Work and Leisure.* New Haven, Conn.: College and University Press, 1963.

Stoppard, Tom, *Rosecrantz and Guildenstern are Dead.* New York: Grove, 1967.

Strauss, Anselm L. and Barney G. Glaser, *Anguish.* Mill Valley, Calif.: Sociology Press, 1970.

Sudnow, David, *Passing On: The Social Organization of Dying.* Englewood Cliffs, N.J.: Prentice-Hall, 1967.

Swados, H., "Less Work—Less Leisure," *Mass Leisure,* edited by E. Larrabee and R. Meyersohn. Glencoe, Ill.: Free Press, 1960.

Taber's Cyclopedic Medical Dictionary. Philadelphia: F. A. Davis, 1970.

Tibbitts, Clark, ed., *Handbook of Social Gerontology.* Chicago: University of Chicago Press, 1960.

——— , "Origin, Scope and Fields of Social Gerontology," *Handbook of Social Gerontology,* edited by Clark Tibbitts. Chicago: University of Chicago Press, 1960.

Tolstoy, Leo, *The Death of Ivan Ilych and Other Stories.* New York: Signet, 1960.

Townsend, Claire, Project Director, *Old Age: The Last Segregation.* New York: Grossman, 1971.

Townsend, Peter, "The Purpose of the Institution," *Social and Psychological Aspects of Aging,* edited by Tibbitts and Donahue. New York: Columbia University Press, 1962.

Tuckman, Jacob and Irving Lorge, "When Aging Begins and Stereotypes about Aging," *Journal of Gerontology* 8 (1953): 489-491.

——— , "Classification of the Self as Young, Middle-Aged, or Old," *Geriatrics* 9 (1954): 534-536.

U.S. Department of Commerce, Bureau of the Census, "Some Demographic Aspects of Aging." Washington, D.C.: U.S. Government Printing Office, 1973.

——— , "Social and Economic Characteristics of the Older Population 1974." Washington, D.C.: U.S. Government Printing Office, 1975.

Valentine, Charles, *A Culture of Poverty.* Chicago: University of Chicago Press, 1968.

Veblen, Thorstein, *The Theory of the Leisure Class.* New York: Mentor, 1953.

Versenyi, Laszlo, *Heidegger, Being, and Truth.* New Haven, Conn.: Yale University Press, 1965.

Wax, Murray, "Tenting with Malinowski," *American Sociological Review* 37 (1972): 1-13.

Wax, Rosalie, "Twelve Years Later: An Analysis of a Field Experience," *American Journal of Sociology* 63 (1957): 133-142.

Weber, Max, *The Protestant Ethic and the Spirit of Capitalism.* New York: Scribner's, 1930.

Weiss, Peter, *Marat/Sade.* New York: Pocket Books, 1965.

Weiss, R. and David Riesman, "Some Issues in the Future of Leisure," *Work and Leisure,* edited by Erwin Smigel. New Haven, Conn.: College and University Press, 1963.

Whyte, W. F., Jr., *The Organization Man.* New York: Simon and Schuster, 1952.

Whyte, William F., *Street Corner Society*. Chicago: University of Chicago Press, second edition, 1955.

Wilensky, Harold L., "Work, Careers and Social Integration," *International Social Science Journal* 12 (1960): 543-560.

——— , "The Professionalization of Everyone?" *The Sociology of Organizations,* edited by Oscar Grunsky and George Miller. New York: Free Press, 1970.

Wolfbein, S. and E. Burgess, "Employment and Retirement," *Aging in Western Societies,* edited by Ernest Burgess. Chicago: University of Chicago Press, 1960.

Wolfe, Tom, *Radical Chick & Mau-Mauing the Flak Catcher*. New York: Bantam, 1971.

Wolff, Kurt H., ed., *The Sociology of Georg Simmel*. New York: Free Press, 1950.

Wright, C. and H. Hyman, "Voluntary Association Memberships of American Adults," *Mass Leisure,* edited by E. Larrabee and R. Meyersohn. Glencoe, Ill.: Free Press, 1960.

Zimmerman, Don and Melvin Pollner, "The Everyday World as a Phenomenon," Understanding Everyday Life, edited by Jack D. Douglas. Chicago: Aldine, 1970.

NAME INDEX